JUST WHAT THE COUNTRY NEEDS, ANOTHER POETRY ANTHOLOGY

JUST WHAT THE COUNTRY NEEDS, ANOTHER POETRY ANTHOLOGY

Edited by James McMichael and
Dennis Saleh

Wadsworth Publishing Company, Inc.
Belmont, California

ISBN-0-534-00137-8
L. C. Cat. Card No. 70-159434
Printed in the United States of America

1 2 3 4 5 6 7 8 9 10---76 75 74 73 72 71

Acknowledgements

Ai: "The Country Midwife: A Day," "Hangman," and "The Color Thief" published with permission from the author. "Cannibal" and "Warrior" reprinted with permission from *Intro #3*, edited by R. V. Cassill. Copyright © 1970 by Bantam Books, Inc.

Michael Benedikt: "The Sky" originally published in *Poetry*, copyright © 1969 by The Modern Poetry Association. Reprinted with permission from the Editor of *Poetry*. "The Student of Wonder," from "Coming and Going," reprinted from *New American Review* by permission of the author. "The Future" reprinted with permission from *Stand*. "The Chest of Energy" first published in *The Paris Review*, Issue No. 43, Summer 1968. Reprinted with permission from the author and *The Paris Review, Inc.*

Robert Bly: "Pilgrim Fish Heads" originally published under the title "A Pilgrim Settlement" in *The Tennessee Poetry Journal*. Copyright © 1969 by Robery Bly, reprinted by permission of the author. "The Teeth Mother Naked at Last"; portions of this poem originally published in *New American Review*, and in *The Nation* under the title "Lies." Copyright © 1969 by Robert Bly, reprinted by permission of the author and *The Nation*. "Johnson's Face on Television" copyright © 1969 by Robert Bly, reprinted by permission of the author. "Water Poverty" and "An Empty Place" copyright © 1970 by Robert Bly, reprinted by permission of the author.

Richard Brautigan: "The Winos on Potrero Hill," "The Quail," "The Pill Versus the Springhill Mine Disaster," "Discovery," and "Adrenalin Mother" reprinted from THE PILL VERSUS THE SPRINGHILL MINE DISASTER by Richard Brautigan. Copyright © 1968 by Richard Brautigan. A Seymour Lawrence Book/Delacorte Press. Used by permission. First published by Four Seasons Foundation in its writing series edited by Donald Allen.

Philip Dacey: "The Stricken Child" reprinted with permission from *The University of Tampa Poetry Review*. "The Lovers" reprinted with permission from *The Back Door*. "Storm" reprinted with permission from *Yankee*. "The Stricken Child" and "Storm" also appeared in THE BEAST WITH TWO BACKS, by Philip Dacey, published by Gunrunner Press.

Glover Davis: "From the Dark Room" and "The Dreamer" reprinted from *The Southern Review* by permission of the author. "Anonymous Phonecalls," "Marking Her for My Own," "Helios," and "Bandaging Bread" published with permission from the author.

Russell Edson: "A Performance at Hog Theater" reprinted from *The Seventies* by permission of the author. "What Mother Means" and "The Cult" published with permission from the author. "The Ox" reprinted with permission from *Chelsea Review*.

John Haines: "The Middle Ages," "A Dream of the Police," and "The Sweater of Vladimir Ussachevsky" reprinted with permission from *Kayak*. "A Poem Like a Grenade" and "The Cloud Factory" reprinted by permission from *The Hudson Review*, Vol. XXII, No. 1 (Spring, 1969). Copyright © 1969 by The Hudson Review, Inc.

Michael Harper: "The Black Angel" originally published in *Poetry*, copyright © 1968 by The Modern Poetry Association. Reprinted with permission from the Editor of *Poetry*. "Elvin's Blues" published with permission from the author. "Fool's Getaway" reprinted from DEAR JOHN, DEAR COLTRANE, by Michael S. Harper, by permission of the University of Pittsburgh Press. © 1970 by the University of Pittsburgh Press. "Clark's Way West: Another Version" reprinted from *The Southern Review* by permission of the author.

Robert L. Jones: "Afternoon" and the selection from "Going Home at Night" reprinted from DOWN AT THE SANTA FE DEPOT, with permission from the publisher, Giligia Press.

The selection from "Our Last Visit" and "Annie" reprinted from *The Southern Review* by permission of the author.

Galway Kinnell: "The Hen Flower" copyright © 1969, by Harper's Magazine, Inc. Reprinted from the December, 1969 issue of *Harper's Magazine* by permission of the author. "Under the Maud Moon" reprinted with permission from *The Iowa Review*.

Philip Levine: "They Feed They Lion" reprinted with permission from 5 DETROITS, published by Unicorn Press, and *Kayak*. "How Much Can It Hurt" reprinted with permission from *Kayak*. "To a Fish Head Found on the Beach Near Malaga" and "¡Hola Miguelin!" reprinted by permission from *The Hudson Review*, Vol. XXIII, No. 2 (Summer, 1970). Copyright © 1970 by The Hudson Review, Inc. "Angel Butcher" reprinted with permission from *Northwest Review*.

Larry Levis: "Fish" reprinted with permission from *Intro #2*, edited by R. V. Cassill. Copyright © 1969 by Bantam Books, Inc. "Bat Angels" reprinted with permission from *Nickel Review*. "The Cycle" published with permission from the author.

Lou Lipsitz: "Cold Water" copyright © 1964 by Lou Lipsitz. Reprinted from COLD WATER, by Lou Lipsitz, by permission of Wesleyan University Press. "The Body" reprinted with permission from *Kayak*. "Nose" and "Heart" reprinted from *New American Review* by permission of the author.

Paul Malanga: "Rites," "Downtown in the Fifties," and "The Tail" published with permission from the author. "Aunt Em" reprinted with permission from *From A Window*. "Not Much Hay" reprinted with permission from *Caterpillar*.

James McMichael: "Janet" published with permission from the author. "The Silk Smith" reprinted with permission from *The Iowa Review*. "Lumberbarks" published with permission from the author. "The Vegetables" originally published in *Poetry*, copyright © 1970 by The Modern Poetry Association. Reprinted with permission from the Editor of *Poetry*.

W. S. Merwin: "Fear," "Second Psalm: The Signals," and "Words from a Totem Animal" from THE CARRIER OF LADDERS by W. S. Merwin. Copyright © 1969, 1970 by W. S. Merwin. Reprinted by permission of Atheneum Publishers. "Fear" and "Second Psalm: The Signals" appeared originally in *The New Yorker*. Reprinted by permission; copyright © 1969, 1970 The New Yorker Magazine, Inc. "Words from a Totem Animal" appeared originally in *The Atlantic Monthly*. Copyright

© 1968, by The Atlantic Monthly Company, Boston, Massachusetts. Reprinted with permission.

Bert Meyers: "Funeral" and "They Who Waste Me" copyright © 1965 by Bert Meyers; the selection from "Madman Songs" copyright © 1966 by Bert Meyers from THE DARK BIRDS by Bert Meyers. Reprinted by permission of Doubleday & Company, Inc. "Homecoming, 1969" reprinted with permission from *Kayak*.

Robert Mezey: "At the Point," "I Am Here," "Song," and "One Summer" published with permission from the author. "In This Life" reprinted with permission from *Kayak*.

Dennis Saleh: "The Chameleon" and "The Return" reprinted from *The Massachusetts Review*, © 1970 The Massachusetts Review, Inc. "Crabs" and "The Unconscious" originally published in *Poetry*, copyright © 1970 by The Modern Poetry Association. Reprinted with permission from the Editor of *Poetry*. "A Guide to Familiar American Incest" reprinted with permission from *The North American Review*.

Herbert Scott: "Picture Puzzle" reprinted with permission from *The Beloit Poetry Journal*. "Babies" published with permission from the author. The selection from "The Apprentice Grave Digger" reprinted from *The Massachusetts Review*, © 1970 The Massachusetts Review, Inc. "The Beekeeper's Wife" reprinted with permission from *Epoch*.

Charles Simic: "Dismantling the Silence," "Stone Inside a Stone," "Forest," and "Bestiary for the Fingers of My Right Hand" reprinted from SOMEWHERE AMONG US A STONE IS TAKING NOTES by Charles Simic, with permission from Kayak Books, Inc. "Poem" reprinted from WHAT THE GRASS SAYS by Charles Simic, with permission from Kayak Books, Inc.

Gary Snyder: "By the Tama River at the North End of the Plain in April," "It Was When," and "Kai, Today" from Gary Snyder, REGARDING WAVE. Copyright © 1968, 1970 by Gary Snyder. Reprinted by permission of New Directions Publishing Corporation.

William Stafford: "Willows" reprinted from *Kansas Quarterly* by permission of the author. "On Earth" reprinted by permission from *The Hudson Review*, Vol. XX, No. 3 (Autumn, 1967). Copyright © 1967 by The Hudson Review, Inc. "Memorandum" reprinted from *The New Yorker* by permission of the author. "At First National" reprinted with permission from *The*

Westigan Review of Poetry. "The Prodigal" published with permission from the author.

Mark Strand: "The New Poetry Handbook" copyright © 1969, by Harper's Magazine, Inc. Reprinted from the January, 1970 issue of *Harper's Magazine* by permission of the author. "Courtship" reprinted from *New American Review* by permission of the author.

James Tate: "Barrels of Wedding Rings," "Up Here," "Fire Dance," and "The Blue Booby" reprinted from ROW WITH YOUR HAIR by James Tate, with permission from Kayak Books, Inc.

Peter Wild: "Kite Man" reprinted with permission from *The Beloit Poetry Journal.* "Quitobaquito" reprinted with permission from *Epoch.* "Haystacks," with permission from *Kayak,* and "An Apology for Wolves" reprinted with permission from THE AFTERNOON IN DISMAY by Peter Wild, copyright © 1968 by Peter Wild and published by The Art Association of Cincinnati, Inc.

John Woods: "Gloss" from KEEPING OUT OF TROUBLE by John Woods, copyright © 1968 by Indiana University Press. Poem first copyrighted 1966 by *Kayak.* Reprinted by permission of Indiana University Press. "The Night of Even Breathing" and "Just Before Morning" published with permission from the author.

Charles Wright: "The Poet Grows Older," "#5" and "#10" from "The Bolivar Letters," and "Piccola Elegia" copyright © 1963, 1969, 1970 by Charles Wright. Reprinted from THE GRAVE OF THE RIGHT HAND, by Charles Wright, by permission of Wesleyan University Press. "Piccola Elegia" was first published in *The New Yorker.* "Entries" originally published in *Poetry,* copyright © 1970 by The Modern Poetry Association. Reprinted with permission from the Editor of *Poetry.*

David Young: "Two for the Hampton Institute" reprinted from SWEATING OUT THE WINTER, by David P. Young, by permission of the University of Pittsburgh Press. © 1969 by the University of Pittsburgh Press. "The Boxcar Poem" and "The Owl" reprinted from *New American Review* by permission of the author. "In Heaven" published with permission from the author.

Introduction by X. J. Kennedy

Late in life, Robert Frost parried a question from his audience, "Mr. Frost, do you think America is going to the dogs?" with the reply: "I'm a rank insider, I can't tell." We are all, I suppose, such perplexed insiders when we read (and try to evaluate) poems as freshly made as those in *Another Poetry Anthology*. The book's modest title deserves a little refutation. Though insiders themselves (and their own poems testify to their commitment), James McMichael and Dennis Saleh have given us an anthology both courageous and highly original. In it, they offer a provocative choice of recent poems from American poetry as they see it happening.

If there are readers, at this late date, to whom "modern poetry" means J. Alfred Prufrock and Frost's *North of Boston,* they will find here occasions for wonder. Over the past twenty years, since the mid-century generation of American poets (Randall Jarrell, Delmore Schwartz, and the early work of Robert Lowell and Karl Shapiro), a furious change in American poetry has continued to accelerate. At the start of the 1970's, we may find it difficult to see where we are unless we look back upon that territory we have abandoned. A comment by another insider may be to the point: not long ago, Robert Creeley, one of the most radical and influential poets to arrive since the mid-century, was talking off the cuff to a class I taught, explaining some of the changes he had seen. Early in his career, Creeley had placed a story in a leading academic review of the 1940's and 1950's; and when the story appeared, he felt that it had been robbed of some quality of its life. It had become, he said, a piece of furniture.

The situation seems different now: most magazines have ceased to be museums and (especially those small, ephemeral, and informal magazines circulated largely among friends) are instead hospitable stopping-places. Creeley's remarks made me recall that era of twenty years ago when most literary magazines were called *Review* (and not *Kayak* or *Caterpillar*), were published on campuses, and in format looked like college catalogues. Each story or poem had to survive a rigorous scrutiny and, if revised to satisfaction, at last was entombed in the magazine, probably to be read by no one but graduate students, full professors, and on-duty librarians.

Since then, several forces have changed the climate. The intelligent young, who no longer believe their teachers and who regard John Milton as a less important poet than anyone alive, eagerly consume new poetry. Largely because of the public appearances of Allen Ginsberg and the late Dylan Thomas, a new emphasis is placed on reading aloud. (It may be, too, that many now prefer live performances and find print boring.) Cheap offset lithography (as Creeley pointed out) has made it easier for a man to start his own magazine. Nor is the publication of poetry books left entirely to New York firms: Lawrence Ferlinghetti, publishing himself and Ginsberg in his widely distributed City Lights Books, has shown that a small press can win a hearing. And the whole revolution in the arts—away from measured formality and "closed form," toward spontaneity and "openness"—has gained respect for a kind of free verse that poetry editors, only fifteen years ago, might have dismissed as unfinished.

What does one expect of the latest American poetry? For any reader who may wish some pointers, let me offer a few generalities. (In doing so, I begin to appreciate Frost's sagacity in keeping his mouth shut about America.) What matters in this latest poetry is truth-telling. The poet strives for absolute fidelity to the emotions he feels, even (at times) piddling, nugatory ones—without concern to place himself in a flattering light. Except for those poems in which he takes refuge behind cool detachment or outrageous humor (and how many of the poems in this book are put-ons and defiances!), he evinces a desperate sincerity. This quality of sincerity is valued more highly than brilliance or craftsmanship. Though many poets care about rhythm, and strive for what they believe to be new cadences, they have small interest in meter; and those poets who care for technique are likely to write in syllabics (three syllables in the first line, say, and seven in the second—generally an odd number, to avoid falling into iambs). Rhyme is considered a vestige of the past, like an elephant-foot umbrella stand. (As far as I can see, no poet in *Another Poetry Anthology* employs rhyme except Bert Meyers, in his ironic "Madman Songs." The desire of poets a generation ago—to arrange a few words into patterns of unbudgable perfection—is no longer keenly felt. And so these poems demand that we concentrate not on their patterns or textures, but on what they say. For the poet, available resources of diction have been enlarged, to take in more of the language of mass media and technology, also a few words that once had to be smuggled into the country. Literary allusion has been largely dispensed with, so that if we meet an unfamiliar name, it may well belong to one of the poet's lovers or relatives.

In some respects, this is a healthier climate for poetry. That high ingenuity that once went into concocting a *Review* poem (often a sestina on a subject from classical mythology, full of chosen symbols, signifying nothing) has given way to an attractive ingenuousness. This is not to suggest that poets have become naive fools, but that they show off less deliberately. Poems tend to sound like immediate happenings, caught in the act of toppling from a mouth. Rare nowadays are those fruit-cakes of image and sound once baked by Gerard Manley Hopkins, which no one else has been able to imitate. In part because of Robert Bly and his campaign to win attention to the work of recent poets in Europe and Latin America, there is much conscious probing of the unconscious, much imagery surreal or visionary. And since the subject matter available to poets has tended to be their own experience (and that which they get from print and television), poetry lately has been long on self-examination and examination of contemporary agonies: war, pollution, violence. All these forces have bred a new species of poem: at its worst, muddled, overweight, didactic, and egocentric; at its best, freer, wilder, more honest, a poetry deeper and wider in its view. If these latest American poems seldom appear to be resounding victories, they are instead like guerrilla skirmishes. Or (perhaps more accurately) like personal declarations of peace in a time when war seems to go on forever.

For the most part, the editors have chosen young poets in their twenties and thirties whose reputations are just now ascending. There are also a few poets of middle years (Philip Levine, Bert Meyers, John Haines, John Woods) who seem newcomers because their earlier work was either neglected or misinterpreted. Appropriately shown here with recent work are Galway Kinnell, Robert Mezey, and W. S. Merwin—all of whom began as stanzaic traditionalists only to shift direction. No doubt two editors living in Manhattan, New Orleans, or Iowa City might have seen the landscape differently. For myself, I can readily think of another dozen poets I would have sneaked in if this book were mine, and the reader may well spy his own flagrant omissions.

Still (as the saying goes), one man's meat is another man's anthology. Anyone who cares for poetry ought to encounter much to delight and startle him here. Among such gratifications for me was Russell Edson, whose terse, sardonic works need to be called poems for want of another label. Another was Richard Brautigan, abruptly popular, whose best work (see "The Winos on Potrero Hill") moves with a beautiful transparency. Here is strong work, too, by such comers as James Tate, Charles Wright, Michael Harper, Charles Simic, and Lou Lipsitz—but I name only a few of the better-recognized. Most of these poems have been caught between book covers for the first time, and the result is a fresh and exciting view of the coming American poetry, a book that well deserves its probable fate: to be burgled by future anthologists.

Preface

For weeks, we talked about what we were going to do with this book, and out of that, what we would call it. We had a contract with a publisher for a collection of contemporary American poetry, and that's all we knew they wanted; all we knew we wanted was a good book. Finally we realized what we were doing, no matter what else we told ourselves: getting ready to begin still another poetry anthology. With that we owned up, and congratulated ourselves on our title.

By then, we also had some ideas about how contemporary the book would be. At the very least, it would contain no poems previously anthologized; if we could satisfy ourselves that we had no such poems when we eventually turned the manuscript in, we wouldn't worry about some other anthology getting back from the printer before ours, with a few overlapping poems. Ideally, we wanted the most recent poems poets had to show. We looked in their newest books and took some, many from books published this year. We looked in magazines they suggested, and found poems that would stay hidden unless they surfaced later in some other book. Finally, and this was the most exciting part, we were shown poems being written, poems we saw change as they approached their final form. We looked at poems only months and weeks old, and by including in our book many poems previously unpublished anywhere, were able to short-circuit the whole long, sad process of getting a poem to its audience.

Other things about our book excited us. We were happy to be including poets never before anthologized, young writers whose work might be of particular interest to others their age. We noted the range of ages, from a 23-year-old student in a writing program to a 56-year-old National Book Award winner. We were happy to be including poets whose names the reader would recognize, with poems by them the reader wouldn't recognize. These were poems from books still being written, that the poets are now reading aloud on their tours of schools and auditoriums. Altogether we were pleased with the immediacy of our book, with its genuine access to contemporary American poetry.

And aside from all that, what could we say about our choices? Indeed, what would determine our decisions? We could worry about representing something, some scheme or notion of American poetry, or we could forget that, since that's how an anthology always builds failure into itself, by pretending to be representative. What we did was put together as fine a book as we could, all considerations aside but the poems themselves. One by one, did we think they were good poems? What we thought is obvious; here is where someone else begins.

James McMichael
Dennis Saleh

June 1970

Contents

JUST WHAT THE COUNTRY NEEDS, ANOTHER POETRY ANTHOLOGY

Ai

The Country Midwife: A Day

I bend over the woman.
This is the third time between abortions.
I dip a towel into a bucket of hot water,
hot water that is already cooling off.
I catch the first bit of blood in the towel,
as the blue-pink dome of a head breaks through
and a scraggy, red man-child comes out of her into
  my hands
like warehouse ice sliding down the chute.

And it's done
and the stink of birth, Old Grizzly,
rears up on his hind legs in front of me.
I want to go outside,
but I know the air smells the same there too.
I look down.
The woman's left eye twitches
and beneath her, a stain as orange as sunrise
spreads over the sheet.
I lift my short, blunt fingers to my face
and I let her bleed, Lord, I let her bleed.

Hangman

In the fields, the silos open their mouths
And let the grain dribble down their sides,
For they are overflowing.
The farmers swing their scythes,
Brows dripping blood.
They have had the passion
Ripped out of their chests
And share no brotherhood with the wheat,

While far across the open land,
The Hangman mounts an empty scaffold.
He slides his hands over the coarse-grained cedar
And smells the whole Lebanese coast
In the upraised arms of Kansas.
The rope's stiff bristles prick his fingers,
As he holds it and lifts himself
Above the trap door.

He touches the wood again.
This will be his last hanging
And anyway he has seen other fields,
Hangmen nailing brass spikes into the scaffolds,
And rope which coiled and uncoiled
In the laps of farm women.
He places his foot on the step going down
And nearby, a scarecrow explodes,
Sending tiny slivers of straw into his eyes.

The Color Thief

I enter your room,
with my purple face moist from excitement.
The black straw basket that I carry
in my yellow arms cracks softly,
in tune with the brittle snap of my blue legs,
as I sneak to your bed.
Little girl, have you got a pink buttock to lend,
or a cream-colored navel
that darkens to brown as it spirals inward?

Or breasts? Yes.
They are swelling now
for the first time.
I touch them.
I take the nipples in my hands.
They are hard
and almost as magenta as plums.
I drop them into my basket
and leave quickly.
The light bulbs that I've stuck in the tips of your breasts
shine far into your middle age,
the clearest white I've ever seen.

Cannibal

You spend your mornings
spitting tiny bones
from your mouth.
At noon, you soak them in milk,
polish them with damask
and carefully lay them
on a black velvet tablecloth.
You think there is nothing so fine
as the reflection of sunlight
on milk-soaked bone
and you stare at them,
recalling the odor of their blood,
the texture of their flesh.
You stroke them.
You love them.
O your wonderful toys.

Already, the bones
have their own secrets
and shine, even in darkness.

Warrior

You sharpen the tip of a spear
with your teeth,
while your wife plows the ground
with the jawbone of an ox.
She is a great, black fire.

The old blood is drifting up your throat
and the witch-men sing all night
of the melon-breasted women in rival villages,
but the spear is wilting in your hands.

When you are standing in the river,
you grab a fish,
tear its flesh open with your teeth
and hold it,
until the bones in your fingers break up
and fly about you like moths.

The river, a fish, your fingers, moths,
the war song churning in your belly.

Michael Benedikt

The Sky

After all this experience, the sky must feel the vast
 potential weight
Some of the birds look lighter than usual but consider
 the seagull lying there now in a ditch at the water's
 edge, like an old rock
When the sky sees the flamingo *en route* it backs off
 in horror, especially at the clumsy ones
It will not even stay in the same room as the ostrich
While hummingbirds fall with a thud
And flies and mosquitoes descend and resemble the
 overtones of clashing cymbals on an oscilloscope

This is why the sky goes around dropping airliners
 all the time:
The sky is tired
It has looked at the Boeing 707 numerous times and
 said "Enough is enough, I can hardly go on
 anymore—but of course I must"
This is to say that it is less like an apprentice
 serving-maid innocently dropping dishes in a
 Bavarian Alp
Than it is like an ancient faithful servant with an
 annoyed look, shaking drops of piss from a pervert's
 favorite mackintosh

That is why I would like to present to this august
 gathering of all the dignified people on earth
A concrete proposal:

Everything must become lighter
All phenomena of flora and fauna
When I reach for my cigarette lighter, for example *(he reaches for his cigarette lighter, lying on the podium)*
I want it to fly away before my hand, since my body has created a breeze *(the cigarette lighter ascends)*
When I am wearing the best clothing money can buy *(he parts his jacket to exhibit his matching tweed vest)*
I want it to be delicate as the web of the spider, the only creature which in the above circumstances is still able to fly, I might add in passing *(his body lights up, and we can see that he is wearing a transparent suit)*
When I am speaking the most profound thoughts, I want them to be both enchanting and thrilling *(he writes this poem)*
And when these thoughts all age, I want to begin to disappear

from Coming and Going

II. The Student of Wonder

There is a book in the head whose pages are constantly
 rustling
When the lamp of solitude is lit we read it by the light of
 silence
Bending over our head, with one finger following the
 lines, the way a roué or rapist will follow a lonely
 night-walking woman down 94th Street
Follow her, until she begins to run
Her feet tapping down the sidewalk and through the
 halls of all these neglected West Side apartment houses,
 sad domains without doormen
And wisdom is achieved, and proclaimed with a stifled
 cry

Meanwhile, the other finger lies on the side of the head.
 As if stuck to it.
It does not move but points perpetually
Indicating to the vital rays that are pressing in from
 without, and space, and the vibrations that are filling
 the room from the Great Nebula in Andromeda
The location of the brain, so that it may be enlightened,
 after several more decades of this.
Late, late, the student of wonder sits at the tables of
 thought and in the chairs of memory, smoking the
 cigarettes of eternity.

The Future

The future is withdrawn again.
Just as the donkey's teeth are pressing against the carrot, somebody removes the donkey.
If this is all the future holds for our nation's donkeys, we may never make it through the forthcoming year!
What we need is a future in which vegetable gardens are planted in the atmosphere.
Gnash gnash.
Each step of the way must be marked by a half-eaten tuber or legume tossed aside, as if luxury were everyday
Or, as if donkeys could not go in any direction they wanted, even into the past.

Advancing on all sides, listen to the delicate steppings and droppings of the donkeys, catching up to the future, making the past come alive sooner and sooner.
When the future is finally achieved, the valley of the world will see, strewn as far as the eye can see, donkeys sitting down or lying around at their ease, little carts unhitched and parked; we will be aware as never before of the portability of time

The Chest of Energy

The energy chest
One keeps dipping in

With the hand of one's head
And one's chest is seldom empty

It's lively.
Even at night when we sleep

We see it
Standing by the bedroom window

Looking out into the distant valley, just standing there
On tiptoe.

Robert Bly

Pilgrim Fish Heads

It is a Pilgrim village; heavy rain is falling.
Fish heads lie smiling at the corners of houses.
Inside, words like "Samson" hang from the rafters.
Outdoors, the chickens squawk in woody hovels,
yet the chickens are walking on Calvinist ground.
The women move through the dark kitchen, their heavy
skirts bear them down like drowning men.
Upstairs, beds are like thunderstorms on the bare floor,
leaving the covers always moist by the rough wood.
And the eggs! Strange, white, perfect eggs!
Eggs that even the rain could not move,
white, painless, with tails only in nightmares.
And the Indian, damp, musky, asking for a bed.
The Mattopoiset is in league with rotting wood,
he has made a conspiracy with the salamander,
he has made treaties with the cold heads of fishes.
In the grave he does not rot, but vanishes into water.
The Indian goes on living in the rain-soaked stumps.
This is our enemy, this is the outcast,
the one from which we must protect our nation,
the one whose dark hair hides us from the sun.

from The Teeth Mother Naked at Last

II

The ministers lie, the professors lie, the television lies,
  the priests lie. . . .
These lies mean that the country wants to die.
Lie after lie starts out into the prairie grass,
like enormous trains of Conestoga wagons. . . .

And a long desire for death flows out, guiding
the enormous caravans from beneath,
stringing together the vague and foolish words.

It is a desire to eat death,
to gobble it down,
to rush on it like a cobra with mouth open,

It's a desire to take death inside,
to feel it burning inside, pushing out velvety hairs,
like a clothes brush in the intestines

This is the thrill that leads the President on to lie

*   *   *

The Chief Executive enters; the Press Conference begins:
First the President lies about the date the Appalachian
  Mountains rose

Then he lies about the population of Chicago, then
  about the weight of the adult eagle, next about the
  acreage of the Everglades

He lies about the number of fish taken every year in the
  Arctic, he has private information about which city *is*
  the capital of Wyoming, he lies about the birthplace
  of Attila the Hun

He lies about the composition of the amniotic fluid, he
insists that Luther was never a German, and insists
that only the Protestants sold indulgences,

That Pope Leo X *wanted* to reform the church, but the
"liberal elements" prevented him,

That the Peasants' War was fomented by Italians from
the North.
And the Attorney General lies about the time the sun
sets.

* * *

This is only the deep longing for death.
It is the longing for someone to come and take us by
the hand to where they all are sleeping:
where the Egyptian Pharoahs are asleep, and your own
mother,
and all those disappeared children, who used to go
around with you in a swing at grade school. . . .

Do not be angry at the President—he is longing to take
in his hand
the locks of death hair—
to meet his own children sleeping, or unborn. . . .

He is drifting sideways toward the dusty places

III

That's what it's like for a rich country to make war,
That's what it's like to bomb huts (afterwards described
as "structures")
That's what it's like to kill marginal farmers (afterwards
described as "Communists")

This is what it's like to watch the altimeter needle going
mad

Baron 25, *this is* 81. *Are there any friendlies in the area?*
81 *from* 25, *negative on the friendlies. I'd like you to*
take out as many structures as possible located in those
trees within 200 *meters east and west of my smoke mark.*

diving, the green earth swinging, cheeks hanging back,
red pins blossoming ahead of us, 20 millimeter
cannon fire, leveling off, rice fields shooting by like
telephone poles, smoke rising, hut roofs loom up huge
as landing fields, slugs going in, half the huts on fire,
figures running, palm trees burning, shooting past, up
again; blue sky, cloud mountains

That is what it's like to have a gross national product

It's because a hospital room in the average American
city now costs $60 a day that we bombed
schoolhouses in the North

It's because the aluminum window-shade business is
doing so well in the United States that we roll fire
over entire villages

It's because the milk trains coming into New Jersey hit
the right switches every day that the best Vietnamese
men are cut in two by American bullets that follow
each other like freight cars

This is what it's like to send firebombs down in 110°
heat from air-conditioned cockpits,

This is what it's like to be told to fire into a reed hut
with an automatic weapon,

It's because we have new packaging for smoked oysters
that bomb holes appear in the rice paddies

It is because we have so few women sobbing in back
  rooms,
because we have so few children's heads torn apart by
  high-velocity bullets,
because we have so few tears falling on our own hands
that the Super Sabre turns and screams down toward
  the earth

It's because tax-payers move to the suburbs that we
  transfer populations.
The Marines use cigarette lighters to light the thatched
  roofs of huts
because so many Americans own their own homes.

IV

I see a car rolling toward a rock wall.
The treads in the face begin to crack.
We all feel like tires being run down roads under heavy
  cars.

The teenager imagines herself floating through the
  Seven Spheres.
Oven doors are found
open.
Soot collects over the doorframe, has children, takes
  courses,
goes mad, and dies.

There is a black silo inside our bodies, revolving fast.
Bits of black paint are flaking off,
where the motorcycles roar, around and around,
rising higher on the silo walls,
the bodies bent toward the horizon,
driven by angry women dressed in black.

* * *

I know that books are tired of us.
I *know* they are chaining the Bible to chairs.
Books don't want to remain in the same room with us anymore.

New Testaments are escaping! . . . Dressed as women . . . they go off after dark.
And Plato! Plato. . . . Plato wants to go backwards. . . .
He wants to hurry back up the river of time, so he can end as some blob of seaflesh rotting on an Australian beach.

V

Why are they dying? I have written this so many times.
They are dying because the President has opened a Bible again.

They are dying because gold deposits have been found among the Shoshoni Indians.

Because money follows intellect!
and intellect is like a fan opening in the wind—

The Marines think that unless they die the rivers will not move.
They are dying so that mountain shadows can fall north in the afternoon,
so that the beetle can move along the ground near the fallen twigs.

VI

But if one of those children came near that we have set
  on fire,
came toward you like a gray barn, walking,
you would howl like a wind tunnel in a hurricane,
you would tear at your shirt with blue hands,
you would drive over your own child's wagon trying to
  back up,
the pupils of your eyes would go wild—

If a child came by burning, you would dance on a lawn,
trying to walk into the air, digging into your cheeks,
you would ram your head against the wall of your
  bedroom
like a bull penned too long in his moody pen—

If one of those children came toward me with both
  hands
in the air, fire rising along both elbows,
I would suddenly go back to my animal brain,
I would drop on all fours, screaming,
my vocal chords would turn blue, yours would too,
it would be two days before I could play with my own
  children again.

VII

I want to sleep awhile in the rays of the sun slanting
  over the snow.
Don't wake me.
Don't tell me how much grief there is in the leaf with
  its natural oils.
Don't tell me how many children have been born with
  stumpy feet
all those years we lived in Augustine's shadow.

Tell me about the dust that falls from the yellow
daffodil shaken in the restless winds.
Tell me about the particles of Babylonian thought that
still pass through the earthworm every day.
Don't tell me about "the frightening laborers who do
not read books."

Now the whole nation starts to whirl,
the end of the Republic breaks off,
Europe comes to take revenge,
the mad beast covered with European hair rushes
through the mesa bushes in Mendocino County,
pigs rush toward the cliff,
the waters underneath part: in one ocean luminous
globes float up (in them hairy and ecstatic men)—
in the other, the teeth-mother, naked at last.

Let us drive cars
up
the light beams
to the stars. . . .

And return to earth crouched inside the drop of sweat
that falls again and again
from the chin of the Protestant tied in the fire.

Johnson's Face on Television

It is a stomach with eyes, something
that moves along the ground, eating,
glancing up, occasionally,
to look at the light.

It is a shovel without a handle,
digging down, throwing up dirt
steadily, doing well now,
almost down to the grave.

Water Poverty

Living daily with less than the average person considers necessary for comfort is not called poverty, but water-poverty. Water doesn't like high places, and tries to get out of them. It is content to live where no one else wants to live, in sloughs and hollows of stubble fields.

An Empty Place

Empty places are white and light-footed. "Taking the road" means being willing to die like the pigeon grass clump that dies so quietly. There is a joy in emptiness. One fall day I saw an empty corncob on the ground, so beautiful, and where each kernel had been, there was a place to live.

In fall privacy we see things clearly:
the dusty ground,
small pieces of crushed oyster shells,
like doors into the earth made of mother-of-pearl;
slivers of glass,
a white chicken's feather that still seems excited by
  the warm blood,
and a corncob, all kernels gone, room after room in
  its empty palace—
this is the place of many mansions
which Christ has gone to prepare for us.

Richard Brautigan

The Winos on Potrero Hill

Alas, they get
their bottles
from a small
neighborhood store.
The old Russian
sells them port
and passes no moral
judgment. They go
and sit under
the green bushes
that grow along
the wooden stairs.
They could almost
be exotic flowers,
they drink so
quietly.

The Quail

There are three quail in a cage next door,
and they are the sweet delight of our mornings,
calling to us like small frosted cakes:
   bobwhitebobwhitebobwhite,
but at night they drive our God-damn cat Jake crazy.
They run around that cage like pinballs
as he stands out there,
smelling their asses through the wire.

The Pill Versus the Springhill Mine Disaster

When you take your pill
it's like a mine disaster.
I think of all the people
lost inside of you.

Discovery

The petals of the vagina unfold
like Christopher Columbus
taking off his shoes.

Is there anything more beautiful
than the bow of a ship
touching a new world?

Adrenalin Mother

Adrenalin Mother,
with your dress of comets
and shoes of swift bird wings
and shadow of jumping fish,
thank you for touching,
understanding and loving my life.
Without you, I am dead.

Philip Dacey

The Stricken Child

Enter her foot
With the doctor who
Cuts through
To the bone, baring

To put right
The way the deep
White web
Hangs together.

Move with the light
As it sings on
The tracery of bone
And living wire,

And feel how
The miles of thin
Fingers inside
Could pull tight

The net so
Delicately spread
Through her twelfth-
Year body.

Then imagine her
Only space
Drawing shut
And you within

Witnessing how
Death and beauty
Flash there
Along thin tracks.

The Lovers

It is exactly right
the way we hold hands.
Animals could not
do it better.
The grip

is not unlike wrestlers'
or a couple's
at a ledge, one
hanging over. No,
we don't sit so

melodramatically, but we aren't
settled either.
Our hands are
an African plain
small beasts

run over.
There's always .
something doing.
As harmless as a helicopter-
safari, perhaps,

or something darker
rushing from the horizon.
See how each hand
keeps up with the other,
exchanging looks!

Storm

Fish at the hole
Cut wide in ice
Seem to shiver, stunned
At the sight of snow.

The water loses it
Immediately
But there is no end
To the soft flood.

The fish dive
In disbelief, return
And find it true,
The flakes growing even

Larger, filling
Their unblinking eyes.
Slowly their mouths
Open and shut,

Breathing nothing
Translatable about
This whiteness broken
So beautifully in air.

Glover Davis

From the Dark Room

People buy sun glasses, beer, oil their skins
and change their clothes like elms putting up shields
of green, but still the heat presses. I wince
as every sonic boom shakes trays, and winds

seem to sweep out of the dark; the red that glows
from the ceiling light dances across the waves
until my rubbered hand stops everything.
I see the world in pictures. When light flows

through delicate patterns of leaves or clouds
they stiffen and wait for the thunder. But the film
is there like raw tissue open to the light.
I see in photos, people strung in crowds

on the beaches, in the streets, on the pavements
black with heat where people run and are caught
by bursts of flashbulbs, or where alone and guilty
they turn on their lives in these explosive moments.

They seem the same, unlike the bulbs that heat
has left clouded and split with veins. But I
am here alone as always, feeling fine.
I turn from my work a few times a day to eat.

I noticed yesterday the negative
of school children caught at play, their features
like charcoal, their hair, lips, and eyes a luminous
expanding white, the sky black and tentative.

Anonymous Phonecalls

The girl across the table rattles
    a porcelain cup.
Her fear moves across her eyes like wind
    over water
or her hand across a pane of clear glass.

She takes off her tinted contact
    lenses and her eyes
change color—green beneath silver.
    The black centers
push pencilled islands outward toward
    the whitening edges.

2.

    Sometimes, late at night
she phones me anonymously, and
    I feel her voice slide
like a glass wave and gain momentum.
    Something calls me so
quietly that it's just below anything
    I can hear. It's soft
as flame wearing through cellophane and
    the things that aren't said
pass through the air in needles of silence.

    Her breathing's regular
and smooth. It seems to indicate pain,
    and it comes coursing
over the wires, rippling a long rope,
    one end in her hand
and one end in mine. Her voice
    is rich and deep and
it swells like a column of blood,
    spinning blackened coins
across the disks of microphones,
    circulating strands
of smoke through the hot circles of her throat.

3.

I speak from a pocket of darkness
near the telephone;
echoes come back like sonar,
and I can tell that
she's finished. I can tell that she's let
the blunt receiver
slip from her hand, down the bedspread where
it corkscrews on
the end of the cord, where the great lips char
in the searing wind
that rushes from the mouthpiece.

Marking Her for My Own

I would like to crawl
into the slats of
the fence and warp with
the weather and throw
out an even shadow.

To crumble softly
like a clod of loose
dirt at the pressure
of the first touch would
be the very best thing.

But I live and grow
more skin. The giant
trees put on a hundred
years with every ring
of bark and I am
so circled with my
own husk that it is
only through pain—the
soft reflection of it
working on your face—
that I can see myself.

2.

I would like to take
alcohol and sponge
your arm or even
the bottom of your feet
and print your white skin
with a blue tattoo
and enter the swollen
ridges of skin and
suffer the puffing of
the scabs and heal with you.

And you could live with me,
indelibly marked
like a sacrament,
and feel the patch of skin
and the delicate lines
that I have made
for you. At night you
could take the tips of
your fingers and touch
the welts on the bottom
of your feet and watch
the pigment glow and
course through your skin.

The Dreamer

for G.M.E.

Sitting, watching, hoping for something new,
he put his cup against the light as if
it were a negative. He saw the blue

white china cup within his hand begin
to pulse, the rim expand, and whiten at
the mouth, until the bridge, the stunted pine,

and the twisted cypress stretched before him
like a dream. He heard the tinkle of the wind
in the glass trees and tore pebbles from the limb.

He came to the great pagoda with its blue tower
and climbed to where the sky meets the designs.
He saw above his head the pale flower

and tore some petals loose and ate, looking
for doors or windows where there were only
the painted panels and more roofs. Locking

his fingers in the quilted leaves he climbed
up past the timberline to the icy slopes
and saw, below, the coffee stream like lead.

He dropped a pebble in the pool and felt
the circles like the targets of his eyes
extend to the cupped white skin and melt.

Helios

1.

In the mountains east of San Diego
the high grass whispers.
After a month of rain, the fields
are shocked with mustard, and wild lilacs.
Acorns caught in the crevices of burnt oaks
bloom from the dead branches
and turgid summer, hazed, sweet, white
summer comes again brazing the hair of the grass.

2.

In the fierce rush of things
from the center, sap and honey, ground water
steeped in granite, wax pods split
tongues leak pure air.
The teeth of flowers scissor
upturned trembling bees and clouds
of crimson jostle half an inch above
the fan shaped petals.

3.

The mountain, green jade mountain, rides
the storm of color, imperial and calm;
fire trails touch off lungs, heart
the rippling trails of blood
under my skin, sobs,
swells of muscle,
undulations pouring inward on the startled eye
unshaken by dynamite, sourced like a mountain.

4.

Holocaust of mouths: pointed
chattering tongues of plants
drift from burning odors of leaves.
By noon the flank of the mountain is an acre
of swaying tongues, nature's poor, circling
an eternal stem; driven by the blazing wind
toward pools of gleaming asphalt on the road below.

5.

Bulldozer, tracthouse, dynamite
5 yrs. away and the imagination flutters
a burnt rag of surrender above the city.
Dusk and the light comes in
over slopes, boulders. Shadows pool
the purples and the greens. Below us
white flocks of pigeons dot
rising blooms in a meadow of air.

6.

The mad, red hair of the poppy
floats toward the sun. Its stem, an anchoring
torso. It tugs like a blimp.
Ten of them in my hand; the red pulse grains
my arm. My head is magnetic for blood.
I pray to the roots of the oak.
Helios in the blood
in the last drunken daze of sun.

Bandaging Bread

for Leon

"Police will cluster
along the borders of the ghettos.
The precincts will pulse like wounded flies.
People are burning," L says,
"everything rocks in a film of heat."
He lifts two loaves of black bread
from the map on his kitchen table.
"This bread is taped like dynamite
for the C.I.A. is everywhere
and we must practice.
The time is coming,
we cannot hold it back,
when the wounds of the table
will swell like blossoms.
The time is coming," he says
pointing to a bridge,
"a loaf here,
and the bridge will rise like dust,
the suburbs will settle and fill with light."

Russell Edson

A Performance at Hog Theater

There was once a hog theater
where hogs performed as men might
had men been hogs.

One hog said
I will be a hog in a field which has found a mouse
which is being eaten by the same hog
which is in the field
and which has found the mouse;
which I am performing as my contribution
to the performer's art.

Oh let's just be hogs, cried an old hog.

And so the hogs streamed out of the theater
crying
        only hogs
                only hogs.

What Mother Means

There is a woman who breaks windows—Yes she does!
My mother allows that this is likely not the entire
periphery of what the woman must own to.

You mean, mama, the perimeter of her entire conduct
must encompass more than direct blame accounts for?

I mean, said mother, the circumference of her activities
must flesh more than window breakage.

In other words, were the full profile known, window breaking
would seem the least of her moral impediments? I said.

I mean, said mother, should the full silhouette,
the entire coastline, the total horizon be known
we should find, in comparison, window breaking
more a blessing than the crime it now seems.

You mean the whole outline of her commitment, I said.

You know what I mean, mother screamed.

The Cult

We had mounted long sticks vertically on our hats
with shrouds attached to our shoulders.

Are we odd?

No less so than the circumstances that make us odd.

We are infested with angels
who take the air as their private road
swimming between us and our objects.

It does not do to see genitalia floating in the air
as their gowns blow up.
It is distressing to us who are earning Heaven
to be upset by their innocence.

No
it is best that we wear these poles of virtue
on our hats to ward off these attacks of innocence
lest we lose Heaven.

In Heaven there is no lust.
In Heaven is the barrier.
In Heaven men as angels need never die.

On earth men must wear sticks to keep
the birds of Heaven from stealing Heaven.

As evening falls the doctors herd all of us
who wear sticks on our hats together
to tell us that we need not wear our sticks.

There are
they say
no angels
that
we make ourselves sick with sexual guilt.

But we know that even they wear sticks on their hats
and we forgive them this
for they are only men.

The Ox

There was once a woman whose father over the years had become an ox. She would hear him alone at night lowing in his room.

The change had been so gradual it was hard to say exactly when he was no longer a man, or more ox than man.

It was only one day when she looked up from her dish and looked straight into his face that she noticed that he was an ox.

She cried, you're an ox.

And he began to moo with his great pink tongue hanging out of his mouth.

She could not help noticing (although she fought it) his sexual appointments, as well as his split hooves and horns.

He would stand over the newspaper, turning the pages with his tongue, while he evacuated on the rug.

When this was brought to his attention he would low with sorrow and climb the stairs to his room; and there spend the night in mournful lowing.

John Haines

The Middle Ages

Always on the point of falling asleep,
the figures of men and beasts.

Faces, deeply grained with dirt,
a soiled finger pointing inward.

Like Dürer's Knight, always haunted
by two companions:

the Devil, with a face like a matted hog,
disheveled and split;

and Death, half dog, half monkey,
a withered bishop with an hourglass.

There's a cold lizard underfoot,
the lancehead glitters in its furry collar;

but it's too late now to storm the silence
on God's forbidden mountain.

You have to go on as the century darkens,
the reins still taut in that armored fist.

A Dream of the Police

It happened about the hour
the December moon went down;
I awoke to a deep murmur,
looking down through years of sleep
on a snowlit public square.

A crowd of people surged across
that space toward a building
that kept retreating into the distance.
They carried some grievance,
a petition to the deafened audience
behind those disappearing walls.

And suddenly blocking their way
rode a force of mounted men
whose helmets and buckles flashed
with a wintry light.

I saw a collision of ghosts,
their fury tangled with
the flying shadows of fists
and the wiry lightning of whips.
The horses' flanks clanged
like dull metal, their legs
were like churning wheels;
from loose stones rolled underfoot
traces of white smoke rose
to the sill where I leaned
and stung my eyes.

The people fell back, a field of wheat
pressed darkly under a storm,
and they and the horsemen dispersed
into a grey vagueness of alleys
and windy encampments . . .

And then there was only a silence,
the empty square, by now a prairie
stretching into the stars,
with a few creeping or frozen bodies,
and the stain of blood turning
black in the snow of my sleep.

The Sweater of Vladimir Ussachevsky

Facing the wind of the avenues
one spring evening in New York,
I wore under my thin jacket
a sweater given me by the wife
of a genial Manchurian.

The warmth in that sweater
changed the indifferent city block by block.
The buildings were mountains
that fled as I approached them.
The traffic became sheep and cattle
milling in muddy pastures;
I felt around me the large
movements of men and horses.

It was spring in Siberia or Mongolia,
wherever I happened to be.
Rough but honest voices
called to me out of that solitude:
they told me we are all tired
of this coiling weight,
the oppression of a long winter;
that it was time to renew our life,
burn the expired contracts,
elect new governments.

The old Imperial sun has set,
and I must write a poem to the Emperor.
I shall speak it like the man
I should be, an inhabitant of the frontier,
clad in sweat-darkened wool,
my face stained by wind and smoke.

Surely the Emperor and his court
will want to know what a fine
and generous revolution begins tomorrow
in one of his remote provinces . . .

A Poem Like a Grenade

It is made to be rolled down
a flight of stairs,
placed under a guilty hat,
or casually dropped into a basket
among the desks
of the stolid statesmen.

As it tumbles on the carpeted stairs
or settles quietly
in its wire-wicker nest,
it begins to unfold,
a ragged flower whose raw petals
burn and scar . . .

its wastepaper soil catches fire,
the hat is blown from its hook.
Five or six faces are suddenly,
permanently altered . . .

those minds are changed for good.

There will be many poems written
in the shape of a grenade—
from the hard bits of metal given off
even a government
might catch its death.

The Cloud Factory

Mountains and cold places of the earth
are no man's garden. Here, for instance,
they make other uses of rain.

First it is beaten into a froth like thin milk, then spun
into something like the fleece of angels.
Stretched and wrung out over alpine basins,

it is wadded into bundles,
and these are pitched down the paths
of glaciers—as they fall,
they are shot full of damp stars.

Then the wind comes and carries the clouds
away into valleys and harbors.

And all this takes place in an atmosphere
of wrapped sounds, like the silence of bandages.

A magpie is the bird of this world,
watchman of the cloudworks.
Made of black and white holes constantly
disappearing into one another,
he treads with difficult dignity,
the iridescence of his office
smothered in a bag of grey feathers.

Michael Harper

The Black Angel

Childhood games,
played without innocence,
and in place of the angel,
take me to a grove of pepper trees;
they lighten my head.
Trees emit their odors,
a natural oxygen tent;
have you noticed the air is heavy
in trees that shed their leaves
without hesitance,
and flow with sap,
and are closest
to the angel's skin;
the eyes, each singly
wide, smarting, unreadable
as the sap, and which
recount the games,
verses, puzzles of other men:
I am reading poems
to this black angel.
Kindled in the shrill
eloquence of other men,
the angel forces open my hands
and in the palms
leaves her footprints.

Elvin's Blues

for Elvin Jones

Sniffed, dilating my nostrils,
the cocaine creeps up my
leg, smacks into my groin;
naked with a bone for luck,
I linger in stickiness,
tickled in the joints;
I will always be high—

tired of fresh air,
the stone ground bread,
the humid chant of music
which has led me here,
I reed my song:

"They called me the black
narcissus as I devoured
'the white hopes'
crippled in their inarticulate
madness,
crippled myself,
drums, each like porcelain
chamber pots, upside down,
I hear a faggot insult my
white wife with a sexless grin,
maggots under his eyelids,
a candle of my fistprint
breaks the membrane of his nose.
Now he stutters."

Last Thursday, I lay with you
tincturing your womb
with aimless strokes I could not feel.
Swollen and hard the weekend,
penitant, inane
I sank into your folds,
or salved your pastel tits,
but could not come.

Sexless as a pimp
dying in performance
like a flare gone down,
the tooth of your pier
hones near the wharf.
The ocean is breathing,
its cautious insomnia—
driven here and there—
with only itself to love.

Fool's Getaway

All over the road
the no-winged geese swim in beams,
their wings whipping the fog;
the fog, the snow, the beams
disappear and birches
grow straight up in clearings
each in cottoned silence.
Because it is my first time
in Oregon, I believe
the eleven o'clock air
is not flooded with animals,
that the animals do not
claim my wife beside me,
that the life she hovers
over is animal also,
beating and clutching
in those trees right there.

Clark's Way West: Another Version

The venereal moon
draws six women
to the Missouri River
where they empty their
beaver pelt children
in great Montana falls
near Indian prairie slope.
From the rattler's rattle
their labor was eased
and the children came
from their collective blindness
to the Shawnee burial ground:
each child is blind.
The earth is not invalid here,
the grizzly slaps at salmon,
and stops, and retreats;
and the children bob
down the falls to the basin below.

Robert L. Jones

Afternoon

My mother's first breath was drawn
from the dry heart of afternoon,
and afternoon inhabits every house of her life.
Always the drawers and closets open
to its wooden spoons
and broken garments, its face smiling up
from all the scuffed shoes.
Always the afternoon is filled with the slow
procession through itself.
Always the air holds its memory,
carrying the odors of 50 years of food
and the grease that cooks it,
the odor of rust in the pits of her arms,
odor of her breasts' diminishing
and the blood that hardens within them.

This is afternoon that never gives way to stillness
when she most needs it to be still.
The half-formed gestures go off from her anyway;
they circle around her, describing the body of afternoon.
This is afternoon that never gives way to night
when she most needs to sleep.
It gives light to her small moons of breath,
and to the daily scars of her ankles and hands,
the scar of her belly,
all shining like candles
for afternoon to find its way back.
This is afternoon that doesn't need morning.

It took my mother's place in the womb.
It has taken my place;
it entered, spread itself out
and became the one moment worth two peoples' lives.

from Our Last Visit

II

Now the night is complete.
It is beneath my clothes,
enters me
and I am filled with its cold, black sky.

Is it the same with you, father?
the same
that now clouds form
and a light snow begins to fall
through this night within me that promises to be long,
soft heaps of it
gathering on the sills of my ribs and hips.

Is it the same with you?
Your hair silver,
the stars of an inner midnight?

from Going Home at Night

II

Here is the emptiness, darkened,
and barely lighted by so early a dawn
that the chill is from the inside.
It takes only a moment
for the smile to etch itself,
for things to settle out there around my shoes,
rising up like scuffed gravestones.

Now the hand whose life-line is so like my own
takes mine.
It leads me out and past my body,
into the world that inhabits hers.

Here is her brother, the barber,
looking up from a Tijuana hotel room,
up from a vision of his wife who was everything,
her heart burst on the kitchen floor,
her eyes still holding the dinner she'd made.
We see her death enter him,
fill his body like oil rising
until the light of his eyes flames up
an instant.
We see his hands changed,
the fingers now petals around two buds of air,
two flowers which bloom now
in another world.

Here is the last of her fathers,
his body at rest at the bottom of a river
that flows from his own heart,
his face staring up astonished that it would ever end,
and astonished
that anyone should come to watch it end.

And her mother whose eyes are closed
and at peace,
whose back has grown straight
and might begin again,
whose hair is the color of earth again
and flesh again an orchard,
whose arms go off now
pulling her death along beneath the soil
to the dry edges of Texas.

Annie

it fell to the women and children to keep
the walls of the public buildings clean of
the flesh and limbs of those hit in the bombing

The thin slap of a finger,
the uneven thud of a whole body, trailing
shoes, watch, rings:

you've heard them all,
and the outline of each as it hit
has its place in your heart

and your heart tells you that each
inhabits that same outline within the wall,
your wall

full of spirits and pieces of spirits.
Here is Philip's ear to whisper good morning to,
Nelly's right hand to shake as you begin.

Annie, each day your eyes burn shut
and you cut yourself,
scraping knuckles on knuckles,

and never complain, seeing that
though its surface grows more pocked
and its body fuller, the wall just takes it.

And when you leave the wall at night,
it is the leavetaking of two friends,
both knowing

that at the end of the war
you will take your place.
Whether in flight

or with a slight step up to miss the shrubs,
you will enter, be met
and a great greeting will go up and float

along the wall as it enfolds you.

Galway Kinnell

The Hen Flower

1

Sprawled
on our faces in the spring
nights, teeth
biting down on hen feathers, bits of the hen
still stuck in the crevices—if only
we could let go
like her, throw ourselves
on the mercy of darkness, like the hen,

tuck our head
under a wing, hold ourselves still
a few moments, as she
falls out into her little trance in the witchgrass,
or turn over
and be stroked with a finger
down the throat feathers,
down the throat knuckles,
down over the hum
of the wishbone tuning its high D in thin blood,
down over
the breastbone risen up
out of breast flesh, until the fatted thing
woozes off, head
thrown back
on the chopping block, longing only
to die.

2

When the ax-
scented breeze flourishes
about her, her cheeks crush in,
her comb
grays, the gizzard
that turns the thousand acidic millstones of her fate
convulses: ready or not
the next egg, bobbling
its globe of golden earth,
skids forth, ridding her even
of the life to come.

3

Almost high
on subsided gravity, I remain afoot,
a hen flower
dangling from a hand,
wing
of my wing,
of my bones and veins,
of my flesh
hairs lifting all over me in the first ghostly breeze
after death,

wing
made only to fly—unable
to write out the sorrows of being unable
to hold another in one's arms—and unable
to fly,
and waiting, therefore,
for the sweet, eventual blaze in the genes,
that one day, according to gospel, shall carry it back
into pink skies, where geese
cross at twilight, honking
in tongues.

4

I have glimpsed
by corpse-light, in the opened cadaver
of hen, the mass of tiny,
unborn eggs, each getting
tinier and yellower as it reaches back toward
the icy pulp
of what is, I have felt the zero
freeze itself around the finger dipped slowly in.

5

When the Northern Lights
were opening across the black sky and vanishing,
lighting themselves up
so completely they were vanishing,
I put to my eye the lucent
section of the spealbone of a ram—

I thought suddenly
I could read the cosmos spelling itself,
the huge broken letters
shuddering across the black sky and vanishing,

and in a moment,
in the twinkling of an eye, it came to me
the mockingbird would sing all her nights the cry of the
  rifle,
the tree would hold the bones of the sniper who chose
  not to climb down,
the rose would bloom no one would see it,
the chameleon longing to be changed would remain the
  color of blood.

And I went up
to the henhouse, and took up
the hen killed by weasels, and lugged
the sucked
carcass into first light. And when I hoisted
her up among the young pines, a last
rubbery egg slipping out as I flung her high, didn't it
  happen
the dead
wings creaked open as she soared
across the arms of the Bear?

6

Sprawled face down, waiting
for the rooster to groan out
it is the empty morning, as he groaned out thrice
for the disciple
of stone,
he who crushed with his heel the brain out of the snake,

I remember long ago I sowed
my own first milk
tooth under hen feathers, I planted under hen feathers
the hook
of the wishbone,
which had broken itself so lovingly toward me.

For the future.

It has come to this.

7

Listen, Kinnell,
dumped alive
and dying into the old sway bed,
a layer of crushed feathers all that there is
between you
and the long shaft of darkness shaped as you,
let go.

Even this haunted room
all its materials photographed with tragedy,
even the tiny crucifix drifting face down at the center of
  the earth,
even these feathers freed from their wings forever
are afraid.

Under the Maud Moon

1

A round-
cheeked girlchild comes awake
in her crib. The green
swaddlings tear open,
a filament or vestment
tears, the blue
flower opens.

And she who is born,
she who sings and cries,
she who begins the passage, her hair
sprouting out,
her gums budding for her first spring on earth,
the mist still clinging about
her face, puts
her hand
into her father's mouth, to take hold of
his song.

2

It is all over,
little one, the flipping
and overleaping, the watery
somersaulting alone in the oneness
under the hill, under
the old, lonely bellybutton
pushing forth again
in remembrance,
the drifting there furled in the dark,
pressing a knee or elbow
along a slippery wall, sculpting
the world with each thrash—the stream
of omphalos blood humming all about you.

3

Her head
enters the headhold
which starts sucking her forth: being itself
closes down all over her, gives her
into the shuddering
grip of departure, the slow,
agonized clenches making
the last molds of her life in the dark.

4

The black eye
opens, the pupil
droozed with black hairs
stops, the chakra
on top of the brain throbs a long moment in world light,

and she skids out on her face into light,
this peck
of stunned flesh
clotted with celestial cheesiness, glowing
with the astral violet
of the underlife. And as they cut

her tie to the darkness
she dies
a moment, turns blue as a coal,
the limbs shaking
as the memories rush out of them. When

they hang her up
by the feet, she sucks
air, screams
her first song—and turns rose,

the slow,
beating, featherless arms
already clutching at the emptiness.

5

When it was cold
on our hillside, and you cried
in the crib rocking
through the darkness, on wood
knifed down to the curve of the smile, a sadness
stranger than ours, all of it
flowing from the other world,

I used to come to you
and sit by you
and sing to you. You did not know,
and yet you will remember,
in the silent zones
of the brain, a specter, descendant
of the ghostly forefathers, singing
to you in the nighttime—
not the songs
of light said to wave
through the bright hair of angels,
but a blacker
rasping flowering on that tongue.

6

For when the Maud moon
glimmered in those first nights,
and the Archer lay
sucking the icy biestings of the cosmos,
in his crib of stars,

I had crept down
to riverbanks, their long rustle
of being and perishing, down to marshes
where the earth oozes up
in cold streaks, touching the world
with the underglimmer
of the beginning,
and there learned my only song.

7

And in the days
when you find yourself orphaned,
emptied
of all wind-singing, of light,
the pieces of cursed bread on your tongue,

may there come back to you
a voice,
spectral, calling you
sister!
from everything that dies.

And then
you shall open
this book, even if it is the book of nightmares.

Philip Levine

They Feed They Lion

Out of burlap sacks, out of bearing butter,
Out of black bean and wet slate bread,
Out of the acids of rage, the candor of tar,
Out of creosote, gasoline, drive shafts, wooden dollies
They Lion grow.
                                        Out of the gray hills
Of industrial barns, out of rain, out of bus ride
West Virginia to Kiss My Ass, out of buried aunties,
Mothers hardening like pounded stumps, out of stumps,
Out of the bones' need to sharpen and the muscles' to
  stretch,
They Lion grow.
                                        Earth is eating trees, fence posts,
Gutted cars, earth is calling in her little ones,
"Come home, Come home!" From pig balls,
From the ferocity of pig driven to holiness,
From the furred ear and the full jowl come
The repose of the hung belly, from the purpose
They Lion grow.
                                        From the sweet glues of the trotters
Come the sweet kinks of the fist, from the full flower
Of the hams the thorax of caves,
From "Bow Down" come "Rise up,"
Come they Lion from the reeds of shovels,
The grained arm that pulls the hands,
They Lion grow.

                                        From my five arms and all my hands,
From all my white sins forgiven, they feed,
From my car passing under the stars,
They Lion, from my children inherit,
From the oak turned to a wall, they Lion,
From they sack and they belly opened
And all that was hidden burning on the oil-stained earth
They feed they Lion and he comes.

How Much Can It Hurt

The woman at the checkstand
Who wishes you cancer

The fat man who hates his mother
The Doctor who forgets

The soup bubbling on the back of the stove
The stone staring into the sun

The girl who kisses her own arms
The girl who fries her hair

The egg turning brown under the spoon
The lemon laughing all night long

My brother in his uniform over Dresden
The single thrill of fire going for the bed

The kindergarten blowing its windows out
Chalk burning the little fingers

The newspaper waiting all weekend
Dozing in rain with the deaths smeared on its lips

The oiling and the loading and the springing
The bullets sucking quietly in their cradles

How much can it hurt in the wood
In the long nerve of lead, in the fattened head

How much can it hurt
In each ration of meat hooked and hanging

In the unfinished letter, the dried open socket
The veil of skin flapping, the star falling

My face punctured with glass
The teeth eating themselves in dreams

Our blood refusing to breathe, refusing to sleep
Asking the wounded moon

Asking the pillow, asking, asking
How much can it hurt

To a Fish Head Found on the Beach near Malaga

I

Flat, eventless afternoon
searching among the stones for nothing
I come upon the fish head.
"Hola!"
Right off, head to head, with this
wide-eyed, unlistening remnant
of dead metal trailing its single
stiff feather of flesh.
We talk of loneliness,
of the fear of stones falling like rain,
hatred of water tumbling out of dreams
and filling our small rooms. Shafts of sand
sifting under doors, filming
first the glasses, then the eyes,
weighing down the lips, the cry.

II

Here, halfway
from home, I discover my head, its hideous
King Tongue going. My good hands explore it,
the hair thinning, the eyes scratched
and hot, that let the lids thump down,
and the poor muscles, unsleeping,
as burned as drawn ropes.
Only the chin happy, hidden in fur.

III

But how good to find companionship
of any kind. Fish head and man head,
communing in their tongue, an iron yawn
out over the waves, the one poem born
of the eternal and always going back.
I throw the fish head to the sea.
Let it be fish once more.
                                        I sniff my fingers
and catch the burned essential oil
seeping out of death. Out of beginning,
I hear, under the sea roar, the bone words
of teeth tearing earth and sea,
anointing the tongues with stone and sand,
water eating fish, fish water,
head eating head to let us be.

¡Hola Miguelin!

I

The night is rising in the young grass—
before noon and the land wind
sways through the fields. Along the trunk
of each blade, a juice rising
toward the pale crown.

I shut my eyes and imagine
a black dried bough of olive.
I bend it. When it gives
with a dry cough
a fine dust rises into our nostrils.

II

She stumbles into the noon—this morning
she was a shy wife—and the young
coarse wine that numbs
her arms and cools the sweat on
her forehead is summer itself.

If she goes forward she does so
from side to side
on her long delicate legs, bearing
herself between them, a faint
musk, a crown of curls, a gift
for the night that is always rising.

Angel Butcher

At sunup I am up
hosing down the outdoor abattoir
getting ready. The water
steams and hisses on the white stones
and the air pales to
thin blue.
Today it is
Christophe. I don't see him
come up the long climb or
know he's here until I hear
my breathing double
and he's beside me smiling
like a young girl.
He asks
me the names of all
the tools and all
their functions, he lifts
and weighs and
balances and runs a long
forefinger down the tongue
of each blade.
He asks
me how I came to this place and
this work, and I tell him how
I began with animals, and
he tells me how
he began with animals. We
talk about growing up and losing
the strange things we never
understood and settling.
I help
him with his robes; he
has a kind of modesty and sits
on the stone table with
the ends of the gown crossed
in his lap.

He wants to die
like a rabbit, and he wants me
to help him. I hold
his wrist; it's small, like
the throat of a young hen, but
cool and dry. He holds
mine and I can feel the
blood thudding in the ring
his fingers make.
He helps me, he
guides my hand at first. I can
feel my shoulders settle and
the bones take the weight, I can
feel my lungs flower as the
swing begins. He smiles again
with only one side of his mouth
and looks down to the
dark valley where the cities
burn. When I hit
him he comes apart like a
perfect puzzle or an
old flower.
And my legs
dance and twitch for hours.

Larry Levis

Fish

The cop holds me up like a fish;
he feels the huge bones
surrounding my eyes,
and he runs a thumb under them,

lifting my eyelids
as if they were
envelopes filled with the night.
Now he turns

my head back and forth, gently,
until I'm so tame and still
I could be a tiny, plastic
skull left on the

dashboard of a junked car.
By now he's so sure of me
he chews gum,
and drops his flashlight to his side;

he could be cleaning a trout
while the pines rise into the darkness,
though tonight trout
are freezing into bits of stars

under the ice. When he lets me go
I feel numb, I feel like
a fish burned by his touch, and turn
and slip into the cold

night rippling with neons,
and the razor blades
of the poor,
and the torn mouths on posters.

Once, I thought even through this
I could go quietly as a star
turning over and over
in the deep truce of its light.

Now I must
go on repeating the last, filthy
words on the lips
of this shrunken head,

shining out of its death in the moon—
until trout surface
with their petrified, round eyes,
and the stars begin moving.

Bat Angels

Sometimes they smear the evening on the air
with wings that
sound like piston slap, just noticed.

In the loose fur
their arm-pits fold like rags,
they leave nose-bleeds on snow, and fall
like hands dropped on shoulders.
  I saw one lift straight up turning to light.

  Sometimes, out for itself,
an angel like this
comes twisting with its dead-pan face
and skitters its blind jaws for meat
over the wind and weeds.

It can't be caught, it's mad,
all night it wants
to chew its own blood and whimper and forget
  the flesh it drags—

while the bare rafters tick under the moon.

The Cycle

Tonight cows
are standing absolutely still
grass stirs under them
somewhere

as I go on tying
my shoes
quietly just before daybreak
and you are

opening your blue eyes happily
and I find myself
jumping up and down very softly
or turning somersaults

What could be simpler
than this life
we are leading gently by the halter
to waters that

are turning so clear and true
they keep vanishing altogether
leaving the grass
there, and the enormous hooves silent.

Lou Lipsitz

Cold Water

Cold water on my bare feet.
You are like cold water.

All day I've watched the water
run from the tap, splash into the bushes
where the earth awaits it
and sucks it up.

Cold water! The grass exclaims.

The Body

The body is not much
—a black vase with a thin
neck
that can't hold even
three reeds

—an old ring
on the finger of a widow

Still I've watched
my feet many times
and I've dreamed
of hair that the late sun
passes through

and I've rocked
in my body like an infant
in his father's arms
and like a troubled man
who begins to feel
the earth turning

And I live in my fingers
—dark alleys
that come to a dead end

I cry out that I live
in the alleys of my fingers
each with
its dead end.

Nose

How powerful the nose began
like a trumpet
blowing inward
and we followed its
delicate roar everywhere
over the ground

it blew the fire and smoke
into our brains
and from it, close to the forest floor,
the knowledge of decay
sank into our hearts

we were like dogs then
not hesitating to sniff
the lovely, black acidity of the genitals
and also the scattered manure of our own kind
that told us
we were not alone

but then as we stood up
it was no longer decisive
it became the joke
we came to overrule it
to pick at it to turn away from
what it told us of our own bodies:
what it is
that makes us suddenly break into a sweat

still at times
some difficult
perfume
resurrects the trumpet
and it blows into the forehead
and into the cheeks
and the skull's ancient stones
move
and the lips feel as if
they are about to grasp
a breast's milky nipple

and we follow the small general
without pants
leading
naked irregulars against
the alien, beautiful armies of uprightness.

Heart

The heart has medieval
persistence
and pumps out
blotchy tapestries
of thrones
and forests

to prove fidelity
it can chew up
mouthfuls
of stained glass
sending them
ringing into the blood
like
a knight falling from a turret

it never hesitates
it comprehends armor
it sustains the double beat
of the victor's horse
in the stone courtyard
of the vanquished

it is blind
and its burnt-out sockets stare
as in a starving
face at a dungeon window
yet it
survives
the rack and the whip
only to kill
itself because the lady's body
is consumed under another's hands

if allowed its own way
it will live for long periods
as an infant
but it is also
the only one
who can locate
the child quicker than the wolves.

Paul Malanga

Rites

in his hand he held
the season's first corn
that took so long (nights
went by, and the field
worried him, the way
the wind knocked stalks
down) to be over
with, his wife at his side
and the storage barn
as third partner, red rosin
still on her hands
from painting (she counted
the strokes, the different
colors of the sky,
watched him and heard
the children cry) so that
none of it would dry
or dampen, it meant a
lot (from the mail and
magazines there were new cars,
new clothes, shades of fall
for an evening of town,
cranberry, hayride brown
all for the finely
dressed), yes, a lot, the
buyer to come soon,
and they held it up
and both smelled it, held it
up to the sun, prayers (it
is foolish not to thank
someone for a good year,
crop dusters, god,
chemical men from new
york, mention them all)

watching the noon sun,
the energy of all those days,
of tending and the times
yet to come (last minute
tornadoes, thieves, the
tired pickers and
bargaining) but with
what was given up
behind them, they threw
the first ear at their feet,
the dust not spotting
its sheen, their knowing
where they were, and why
for the best (at best
a trip to des moines,
omaha, maybe chicago before
they began again and tended
more and) they accepted
as humility, an obligation,
as feeders must have,
the corn coming up out of
the earth and all things
else, before it, they cannot
change, the staple crop
(as it is with every
generation and the luxury
the mails permit can bring
no slack, no time for
futility, forgetting the fall
fashions, damn the dyed fabric,
the latest cologne) there is
the air, always, fresh at evening
and birds, always, especially
at nightfall, and the next
years must come (they must).

Aunt Em

"When Aunt Em came there to live she was a young, pretty wife. The sun and wind had changed her, too." *The Wizard of Oz*

1. nebraska

knowing that kansas made flat
fifteen miles away, i could almost
smell the border, rain imminent
in the west and south, and see
the imperfect lights of farm towns
reflected in the sky for as far
as kansas sky might go;
the wind, coming out the belly of a land
in the north, blew on, blew
on and brought the rain; but by
that time i had left one state
and was drawn into another by road-
signs, maps, and shapes of
high mountain firs;
prairie straw piled in
layers from the kansas i had sensed,
and women grew out of nothing
to take it in for winter,
leaving me dust and exposed.

2. colorado

there is but one song
to be sung in these mountains, it is
not the song of melting snow
nor the melody of thin pines;
it is an ever green one and trying
to shape it on the lips, to push
it through the larynx is not
possible: to sing it one must
distend, distend terribly
so that all tension snaps,
and then sing it, floating.

3. arizona

i constructed myself
out of environment:
i took cactus
spines for bones,
flowers out of cactus
for face, and for voice
and mind the thin
water on the rivers.
i left for the east
early in my life
and became kansas
upon entering kansas
there i remained, barren
but beautiful, men
planted me with wheat
and children flew
kites in my wind
but the day was when i knew
i had gone nowhere,
that i had lain, sallow
and cheating to the people;
i bent the calico
from my eyes and pushed
metal silos
off my chest; and while
in colorado, my knees
shook greatly, frightened
by the cloying heights
i fell into the desert,
intense sun
upon my fevers.
and began there to remove
myself from the past,
flowers first,
and turning the water
back to the rivers.

Not Much Hay

The mule out there, a bowed strider
on the sun browned, tramped field
lets his head hang. The heat draws out his tongue
and holds back his voice, and mine,
as we move aimlessly
on the wind shifted ground,
I toward the riverbed,
he in the confines of barbed wire.

We the animals, in the sun's house,
pacing our lives to the place our eyes drop:

this place
with lots topped with old leaves,
anthills opened up, cones and midholes open,
and a strong eucalyptus smell,
and its leper's bark, spotted, stripped, dead tree,
on the roadside.

We stand above:
below our feet, our hooves, goes back to the earth:

old shredded Kotex, like a crumbling, senseless cereal;
what was a horned toad, smashed, tire after tire;
silver and green phosphorescent entrails in mid-
  afternoon's light;
crumpled daiquiri cans, and cacti fruit, and stems,

and I move to the dry river
to turn back, by the prosperous houses,
to wonder about a water tower, dull metal,
in the heat that drains the old mule's balls,

to hang my head.

Downtown in the Fifties

The shoe section of this store
was the heart of merchandise;
cheap but nice brown shoes for the poor,
and other rows, some fancy, or for utility;
I was so young that sales and buyers
weren't even on my mind,
not in that carnival:

two monkeys lived there in a bamboo cage,
a parrot squawked at shoppers,
red and white plumes ruffling,
lifted by the air cooler's wide stream;
and, the best, an old fluoroscope, plated with copper,
showed us our bones, real bones,
in a green glow
to be outlawed, unsafe,
in years to come.

Always the front windows were wide open to the sun,
the doors wide to the tropical breezes,
straw hat weather,
gone weather,
the show packed up by time,
a wink, a dream,
tails, feathers, my spreading white toes;

if you were sold
you walked away
and the whole world came with you.

The Tail

A dead rat, frozen, had curled on its side
sometime during the night.
Foggy morning shrouded the land:

as I picked it up by the tail
and put it in a paper sack
I saw the quarter moon fangs, the ivory,
luxuries in the land of the dead.
Where did it come from and what for?

Around the side of the garage
a love bench stands,
under a vine arbor
where the moon passes,
often yellow,
or a star sinks,
or a rat comes crawling through the smoky dew
and drops like an ugly petal.

James McMichael

Janet

All the bakeries have closed.
The women of the bakeries
Must find something to do.
They clean the sidewalks
Until the sidewalks are as clean
As the floors of bakeries.

They go into the homes of the sick.
They go into the elevators.
With their good smells, they go
Into the parks, and everyone
Follows them there. No one is left
To be sad or talk of harm.
There are flowers, and candles,
And over their own singing

They hear her coming to them
Like a flood of moths, a powder
Of small wings, and she settles
Everywhere, on all faces,
Janet, her heart opening.

The Silk Smith

His hands are not together
But you think of them that way.
They are the cocoon.
Inside, all the threads are pulsing.
He worries the knuckles into fires.

You have brought him
Whatever you would have him touch.
You hope he will bless it,
Will make it fine and strong,

Will make for it a place where no one dies,
Where no one whispers that anyone
Is dying. He can do this, you tell him,
And he seems to hear you,
For you see that his hands

Are not together. They are at his sides.
You can see the backs of them.
You have watched him for a long time.
His hands are at his sides.

Lumberbarks

No one is here
To tell the boats not to think of wood.
It is winter
And everyone is inside.

The wood is outside.
It is on the docks
And the docks are of wood.
The sawmills and warehouses
Are of wood. There is wood
In the trees and the trees are outside.

The snow has made everything very still.
The water does not rock the boats at all
And they think nothing of their moorings.
They will go among the trees.

They move away from the docks,
Going alone
Either up the sound, or down.

There is much fog.
They do not find the rivers easily.
Their rigging is stiff with frost
And they hope soon to feel their decks buckle,
Their masts and spars bloom with a thousand cones.

The Vegetables

E.L.M., 1900-1951

The Artichoke

She bore only the heart,
Worked at the stem with her
Fingers, pulling it to her,
And into her, like a cord.

She would sustain him,
Would cover his heart.
The hairy needles
And the bigger leaves,

These she licked into shape,
Tipping each with its point.
He is the mud-flower,
The thorny hugger.

The Asparagus

She sent packs of great beasts to pass
Over him, trailing belly-fur and dust,
Bending their nostrils to his frail spear.
This was to toughen him. For what?
Stupidly, like a squirrel, standing up,
Looking here and there, looking to all sides,

He is cut down and taken away.
She can smell him steaming, his crowns
Already tender, his spine giving in.
Now he is threatening to wither terribly,
And slip from the water altogether,
And billow through the kitchen like prayer.

The Cauliflower

Her words clot in his head.
He presses himself to remember
And feels the skin peel back,
The skull bleach, crack, fall away.

All that's left of him is the brain,
Its tissue knotting up to shade him,
The pain of its light pulsing
How to move, how to move.

Corn

I am the corn quail.
What I do is quick.
You will know only
The muffled clucking,
The scurry, the first
Shiver of feathers
And I will be up,
I will be in your
Head with no way out,
Wings beating at the
Air behind your eyes.

Herbs

Before fog leaves the scrub-oak
Or the grasses of the downland,
Take dragonwort under the black alder,
Take cockspur grass and henbane,
The belladonna, the deadly nightshade.
Free them as you would a spider's-web,
Singing over them: Out, little wen,
Out, little wen.
Sing this into the mouth of the woman.

Celery

The hope with
water is that it
will conceal nothing,

that a clearness
will follow upon it
like the clearness
after much rain,

or the clearness
where the air
reaches to the river
and touches it,

where the rain
falls from the trees
into the river.

Bell Pepper

To find enough rooms for the gathering
The walls go on alone not waiting
For corners but thinking of sleeves
And how the wind fills them and the snow
Fills them and how cold it is without
Fires when there are not enough rooms.

Potatoes

It had been growing in her like vegetables.
She was going into the ground where it could
Do better, where she could have potatoes.

They would be small and easily mistaken
For stones. It would fall to her to
Sort them out, persuade them to stay

Close to her, comforting her, letting her
Wear them on her body, in her hair,
Helping her hold always very still.

W. S. Merwin

Fear

Fear
there is
fear in fear the name the blue and green walls
falling of and numbers fear the veins that
when they were opened fear flowed from and
these forms it took a ring a ring a ring
a bit of grass green swan's down gliding on
fear into fear and the hatred and something
in everything and it is my death's
disciple leg and fear no he would not
have back those lives again and their fear as
he feared he would say but he feared more he
did not fear more he did fear more
in everything it is there a long time
as I was and it is within those
blue and green walls that the actual
verification has and in fact will
take the form of a ring a ring a ring
took I should say the figure in the hall
of the glass giants the third exhibition
on the right is fear I am I fear and
the rain falling fear red fear yellow fear
blue and green for their depth etcetera
fear etcetera water fire earth air
etcetera in everything made of
human agency or divine fear is
in the answer also and shall pierce thy
bosom too fear three gathered together
four five etcetera the brightest day
the longest day its own fear the light
itself the nine village tailors fear
their thread if not their needles if not
their needles in everything and it is
here this is New York and aside from that

fear which under another name in
every stone Abraham is buried it
is fear the infant's lovely face the
grass green alleys oh at about the third
hour of the night it being in those parts
still light there came fear my loving fear
in everything it is next the baker the
candlestick maker if you know what I
answer at that point and fear the little
cobbler his last is one fear and there is
fear in all shoes in the shoe line the clothes
line any clothes the blood line any in
everything it is the third button
the book books fear the bottle and what it
contains everything a life death the spirit
staring inward on nothing there and
the sunken vessel the path through the shadow
the shadow of me me or if I am not
suddenly fear coming from the west
singing the great song there was no need
fear no crying and others would sift
the salt in silence in fear the house
where I am familiar in all your
former lives remembered your parents
fear and fear theirs of your parents by
your parents and for your parents shall not
perish from this deciding everything
and it is deciding strike out Mr
Mrs Miss I am alone little stones
fear forgetting forgets remembering
it is my loving fear the mouth of my
seeing fear I am awake I am not
awake and fear no bones like my own
brother fear my death's sister and high on
the cliff face the small arched door from which
a man could fear or be in the winking
of an eye the tapping of the second
finger of the left hand the wind itself

fear I am alone forever I am
fear I am alone I fear I am
not alone couldn't tell your breath from fear
for it is your breath I do it and I'm
supposed to explain it too I fear I
completed my fear in everything there is
fear and I would speak for myself but fear
says logic follows but I advance in
everything and so discovery
geography history law comedy
fear law poetry major prophets
minor prophets that pass in the night
it is a mother and a guiding light
moving across fear before which they burn
in rows in red glass bleeding upwards their
hearts smoke in the gusts on earth as it is
in heaven with the sentence beginning
before the heavens were or the earth
had out of fear been called and any began
to be fear the bird feather by feather
note by note eye by eye pierced he is my
neighbor in the uttermost parts of aye
and shall I couple heaven when the fear
shall fear and those who walked in fear shall see
fear their very form and being for
their eyes shall be opened it was going
on in everything and I forgot but if you
stand here you can see fear the new building
starting to rise from which our children
will fear the stilted dogs the insects
who do not exist the dead burning
as candles oh dark flames cold lights in
everything without you the ship coming
in and a long way that I would never
traverse before fear had followed that
scent faster than a mortal bearing fear
I'm telling you I'm asking you I'm dying
I'm here today this is New York I'm more

than any one person or two persons
can stand fear the way down in everything
the way up is the same fear the next place
the next I said fear come on you it's you
I'm addressing get into line you're going
never fear there is a hair hanging by
everything it is the edges of things
the light of things do you see nothing
in them burning and the long crying
didn't you hear that either I mean
you again fear it's a strange name not
for a stranger ma'am he said lying I
mean there is you fear me fear but you
must not imagine fear through which the present
moves like a star that I or that
you either clearly and from the beginning
could ever again because from the beginning
there is fear in everything and it is
me and always was in everything it
is me

Second Psalm: The Signals

When the ox-horn sounds in the buried hills
of Iceland
I am alone
my shadow runs back into me to hide
and there is not room for both of us
and the dread
when the ox-horn sounds on the blue stairs
where the echoes are my mother's name
I am alone
as milk spilled in a street
white instrument
white hand
white music
when the ox-horn is raised like a feather in one
of several rivers
not all of which I have come to
and the note starts toward the sea
I am alone
as the optic nerve of the blind
though in front of me it is written
This is the end of the past
Be happy
when the ox-horn sounds from its tassels of blood
I always seem to be opening
a book an envelope the top of a well
none of them mine
a tray of gloves has been set down
beside my hands
I am alone
as the hour of the stopped clock
when the ox-horn is struck by its brother
and the low grieving denial
gropes forth again with its black hands
I am alone
as one stone left to pray in the desert
after god had unmade himself
I am
I still am

when the ox-horn sounds over the dead oxen
the guns grow light in hands
I the fearer
try to destroy me the fearing
I am alone
as a bow that has lost its nerve
my death sinks into me to hide
as water into stones
before a great cold
when the ox-horn is raised in silence
someone's breath is moving over my face
like the flight of a fly
but I am in this world
without you
I am alone as the sadness surrounding
what has long ministered to our convenience
alone as the note of the horn
as the human voice
saddest of instruments
as a white grain of sand falling in a still sea
alone as the figure she unwove each night alone

alone
as I will be

Words from a Totem Animal

Distance
is where we were
but empty of us and ahead of
me lying out in the rushes thinking
even the nights cannot come back to their hill
any time

I would rather the wind came from outside
from mountains anywhere
from the stars from other
worlds even as
cold as it is this
ghost of mine passing
through me

I know your silence
and the repetition
like that of a word in the ear of death
teaching
itself
itself
that is the sound of my running
the plea
plea that it makes
which you will never hear
oh god of beginnings
immortal

I might have been right
not who I am
but alright
among the walls among the reasons
not even waiting
not seen
but now I am out in my feet

and they on their way
the old trees jump up again and again
strangers
there are no names for the rivers
for the days for the nights
I am who I am
oh lord cold as the thoughts of birds
and everyone can see me

Caught again and held again
again I am not a blessing
they bring me
names
that would fit anything
they bring them to me
they bring me hopes
all day I turn
making ropes
helping

My eyes are waiting for me
in the dusk
they are still closed
they have been waiting a long time
and I am feeling my way toward them

I am going up stream
taking to the water from time to time
my marks dry off the stones before morning
the dark surface
strokes the night
above its way
There are no stars
there is no grief

I will never arrive
I stumble when I remember how it was
with one foot
one foot still in a name

I can turn myself toward the other joys and their lights
but not find them
I can put my words into the mouths
of spirits
but they will not say them
I can run all night and win
and win

Dead leaves crushed grasses fallen limbs
the world is full of prayers
arrived at from
afterwards
a voice full of breaking
heard from afterwards
through all
the length of the night

I am never all of me
unto myself
and sometimes I go slowly
knowing that a sound one sound
is following me from world
to world
and that I die each time
before it reaches me

When I stop I am alone
at night sometimes it is almost good
as though I were almost there
sometimes then I see there is
in a bush beside me the same question
why are you
on this way
I said I will ask the stars
why are you falling and they answered
which of us

I dreamed I had no nails
no hair
I had lost one of the senses
not sure which
the soles peeled from my feet and
drifted away
clouds
It's all one
feet
stay mine
hold the world lightly

Stars even you
have been used
but not you
silence
blessing
calling me when I am lost

Maybe I will come
to where I am one
and find
I have been waiting there
as a new
year finds the song of the nuthatch

Send me out into another life
lord because this one is growing faint
I do not think it goes all the way

Bert Meyers

from Madman Songs

1

People go home
to rest in vaults
curtains soothe their faults
bright windows show their money
I hated home
it caused me pain
cloudy days
and evenings came
I leaned against
the iron rain

2

Someone held me there was harm
now each word's an alarm
the man who looks so calm
will turn into a bomb
Woman daughter son
I wake up and put them on
they hide me from the law
My desire's a blade of grass
I trample as I pass
Fear me what I hate will fall

3

In summer small cones
of dirt beside a fence
erupt with the weddings
of the ants
a moth staggers from a shrub
People turn their sprinklers on
to watch the water girls
dance on their lawn
I don't go out
until they've all gone in
They might come near
with large damp wings
love and other things

They Who Waste Me

When I ask for a hand,
they give me a shovel.
If I complain, they say,
Worms are needles at work
to clothe a corpse for spring.
I sigh. Whoever breathes
has inhaled a neighbor.

Funeral

Surely a dead moth's
the skull of a tiny horse,
and the moon's a saint
who pities the sea.

Peace, peace to this child
of rain and light,
and the people who stay
holding candles and lilies,

tasting their tears,
naked in a dream,
over the long drawer
they've closed in the earth.

Homecoming, 1969

1

My father was a tender man
whose blue eyes would overcast
by noon. Every dusk
he floated home
in the soiled wind of his clothes.

I flew to the ceiling in his arms.
The silverware sang
and the bright room
rolled like a train
climbing its ladder through the dark.

Today, he lies in a bed
near strangers, nursed
by a needle, dissolving in a spoon.

And I imagine coming to him
suddenly, like a song, a son.
I'd bring him to a town
where everyone he cries for now
(wrapped in the bed's thick bandage)
would rush to shake his hand.
He drinks and drinks the meadowlark,
he smoothes a stone's grey hair.

But he stinks, he's a huge bib
from breakfast, lunch, his pants.
A loose scab, a rotten cornflake,
clings to his lip.

2

There are mouths so cold
the salmon-colored tongue
leaps without a sound;
lonely ditches where a broken dove
mourns day and night
in the vacant lot we call a face.

Men, at the mercy of their parts:
grime in the skull, despair
corroding the rainbows in their wires.

3

My home was a watercolor
I left in the rain . . .

Tonight, the crickets ring and ring,
nobody answers;
the shadows of men are looking for blood.

Someone has stepped
on the classical face of the moon.

Dawn comes, a gradual
mountain range of ashes.

4

The mocking-birds, those joyful books
that opened in the sky,
then closed their pages in a tree,
awake and go mad,
chewing the bones of their old songs;
and the flies, such tiny fenders,
batter themselves in the air.

5

My head's a beach full of footprints.

6

I stay among these ruins,
a tired nail trying to hold
an image on a wall that flows away.

Robert Mezey

At the Point

Travelers long on the road
stop here for water and for the view.
Their children run
through the young and old pines,
splashing in the needles
or chasing the wild canaries, their
light cries
receding in the aisles of shade.

The light is so simple
and steady,
as if tiny beaks
had opened a vein of pure sunlight in the forest,
and the fathers and mothers
stand looking down,
their lives
jumping at the base of their throats
and little words
unspoken for twenty or thirty years
cling to their lips like droplets of water.

In the valley the taut fences
stretch pitilessly to the horizon
and all those who want to be someplace else
must follow them.
The hawks and owls crucified on the wire
have long since returned to their own country,
and the mouse trembles in ecstasy,
lost in the shadow of their wings.

In This Life

Now the cup of grasses and down is cool,
the eggs cool, the throne empty
from which she would step down and growing still,
look out long toward the darkness.

One moist and terrible night, it came creeping
and tensing its jaws and it too grew still
and then it had her,
and a small diamond of light opened in her brain.

I remember the eyes closed tight
against the final ecstasy of the teeth,
the weightless blood-beaded lump of feathers buried now
under the iris slowly eaten alive by the air.

Here is the father
blossoming on a twig
to sing the song of the bleeding throat
on this day of crystal wind and young sunlight.

He sings the endless song
of irises wrinkling and wrinkling and becoming nothing,
road of fine sand strewn with fallen wings,
the mouse, the toad, the blind nestling taken in deep
grass,

he sings of a diamond, sings
of the spokes flashing brilliance at the center
of the ceaselessly collapsing floor of bone
and I wish I sang with him,

he sings the only truth
in this world where men remember mostly lies,
sings it and sings it
till it breaks at last into particles of light,

blossoms of mercy
in the midst of the holocaust.

I Am Here

For Naomi, later

I want to speak to you while I can,
in your fourth year before you can well understand,
before this river
white and remorseless carries me away.

You asked me to tell you about death.
I said nothing. I said

This is your father,
this is your father like water,
like fate,
like a feather circling down.

And I am my own daughter
swimming out,
a phosphorescence on the dark face of the surf.

A boat circling on the darkness.

2

She opens her eyes under water. The sun climbs.
She runs, she decapitates flowers.
The grass sparkles. Her little brother laughs.
She serves meals to friends no one has seen.
She races her tricycle in circles.
I come home. The sun falls.

3

You eat all day.
You want to be big. "Look how big!"
you cry,
stretching your arms to heaven,
your eyes stretched
by all the half terrified joy of being in motion.

The big move clumsily, little love,
as far as I can see.
They break everything
and then they break,
and a pool of decayed light sinks back into the earth.

Writing these words tonight,
I am coming to the end
of my 35th year. It means nothing to you,
but I rejoice and I am terrified
and I feel something I can never describe.
They are so much the same,
so much the sun blazing on the edge of a knife. . .

We are little children
and my face has already entered the mist.

4

I hear you cry out
in the blackened theatre of night.
I go in and hold you in my arms
and rock you, watching
your lips working,
your closed eyelids bulge with the nightly vision.

5

I get lost too, Naomi,
in a forest that suddenly rises
from behind my breastbone on a night of no moon.
Stars hang in the black branches,
great, small,
glittering like insoluble crimes,
ceaselessly calling me
toward that thick darkness under the trees.
I turn, sobbing, to run,
but it is everywhere.

6

I wanted to give you something
but always give you something else.
What do you call it when it is underground
like a cold spring in the blood,
when it is a poem written out of naked fear
and love which is never enough,
when it is my face, Naomi,
my face
from which the darkness streams forth?

The petal falls,
the skin crumbles into dirt,
consciousness likewise crumbles
and this is one road the squirrel will not cross again.

I was here, Naomi,

I will never be back
but I was here,
I was here with you and your brother.

Song

Stars overhead
A frog's grunt from the other side of the pond
Clear sound in the summer night

Ollie is asleep
My warm foxy girls
Curled up at my sides
In my lap the story of a king and his youngest daughter

The perfume of hair
Little Omi is breathing the pure breath of sleep

Eve moves to the open door
My senses are full
Of her slim young womanly body
And tinkling anklets

I am ready for sleep

Orion blows like a kite in the summer sky
I think I will climb up his tail
To freedom

One Summer

My father coming home
from the factory
summer and still light out
the green bus at the end
of the endless street
the foul sigh
on which my father stepped down
walking slowly in the shadows
holding my hand
my father tired and frowning
eating his supper of potatoes
reading the Bulletin
news of the war
and columns of boxscores
my father singing lewd hymns
in his tuneless voice
stretched out full length in the tub
his calves hanging over the rim
his long penis resting
on the surface of the grey water

Dennis Saleh

The Chameleon

The chameleon's
real goal
is to get something real
into his life.

All day long he stands
still,
exercising.
He leaps into the air

and lands changed.
He becomes
everything he sees
but isn't: no-leaf,

no-twig,
no-soil. He is always
almost disappearing.
He is the

space of air
at the bottom of a fall,
a huge piece
of money.

Grass. Cloth.
He can even be
another chameleon.
His

is the steady bruise
of use.
He is deciding,
deciding.

Crabs

The crabs lie to themselves.
In a shadow pointing in from the rocks
across low, scrubby grass
they click quietly.
The vacant heat is gone,
water slaps in the growing dark.
Soon the crabs stir, sliding down unhurt.
They skitter down the rocks then hold still,
like broken paper plates or crushed bags.
The dark fine line reaching away frightens them,
the sand shines beneath them.
At the water's edge they start
at water and sand washing past.
Moving up and down the beach
their shadows spindle across weeds and glass,
through patches of light beneath rotting wood.
When they are as far as they ever go they stop,
near the water,
waving and clicking out past themselves.

The Unconscious

Expect the swollen gorge behind everything.
Expect taking in your hands
at least one of your parents
torn open to reveal what is inside.
Expect your conception, the wall you tear away from,
the dark burst ending nothing.
Plan loss. Plan having no room.
Plan slipping to your knees and fear
welling around your knees rising.
Now find the names for everything.
Now talk at last.
Say "Choking," say you are choking,
infancy is choking, childhood is choking,
your body is the throat your blood rushes to
flow from, your body stutters,
now it will never be over.
Realize the rest of your life will be like rain
falling far above you.
Realize Jesus warned you.
Realize you are being lied to,
that at any moment someone will bend to you
and whisper "I was here before you who am I."

A Guide to Familiar American Incest

The Mother

wished to have been milk,
to have passed out of herself entirely,
to have passed out of her nipple.

She searches through herself
for the devil's mark,
the place her son can enter
and not be felt.

Oh if she finds it

The Son

behaves peculiarly,
as if sensing what will fall
to him to do.

If he stands at a window,
he tastes it. His tongue reaches out
hesitantly to touch the glass,
half expecting to press through it
to nothing.

When he passes them,
he is afraid he will press
through his mother,
press through his sister.

He watches his father as though
watching a manta ray
approach him from a closet.

The Daughter

lingers in the bathroom.

She stands on the scale
and imagines how the years
will touch her here, and so,
delicately, like a towel.

Her breath is short, heavy,
a whisper that grows between her legs
like grass to be cut
late in the morning, when dry.

The Father

Everything he says catches
in the air before him,
is a pale and wobbly reflection
nodding gently from his mouth.

He follows it from room to room,
and it crosses and re-crosses
the balloons he sees in everything,
the tense balls of promise.

The father is nothing exacting,
only the suggestion of water moving
through water, parting water.

The Penis

It should be porcelain
and harmless. Or we should
be able to warm our hands at it.

It could warm our hearts.

It will make the air in the room
ring like a bell
and it will beat for an answer.

The Return

I sit in a huge auditorium
behind my father.
I see his ears and study the neck,
the folds there,
like creases of earth,
I watch the grey hair soften
in the still air.
In front of him is his father,
and more fathers, stretching
down in a single row.
While I am counting the fathers,
my father's eyes roll back into
his head and lock on mine.
They stare into me past his brain,
through all the flesh he has managed
and managed to grow for years.
There are eyes staring into him,
eyes staring up
from the dark of the hall.
All the hair is grey,
all the hair is dying,
the eyes say climb down
over the seats, into your father.
All the fathers calling their sons
climb down,
into the hair, save the dying hair,
smooth the creased earth,
kiss the neck.
I stand and don't think.
I touch the father in front of me,
he touches a father,
I climb over the seat.
The hall stirs with all the light
that has gone.
From behind something is rising,
my eyes roll back,
I open my mouth and open my mouth,
like a mouth
yawning and never closing.

Herbert Scott

Picture Puzzle

This piece of sky goes somewhere
above the child's head, the child
with the apple. The sky is blue here,
no clouds in this part of the picture.
But first we must find the child's head.
It is somewhere. We can see the apple
in his hand with the bite missing.
But what is this falling like rain?
There are no clouds. Is it tears, or juice
from the apple? We must find the child's head.
He may be hurt. He may need someone
to find his head. And where is the sun?
Let us look for the sun. There are evidences
of it lighting the wings of birds. Somewhere
there must be a sun, and a child's head
with a bite of apple in its mouth.

Babies

Our houses are full of babies,
babies under beds, between the pages
of books, in the soup. We open
our mouths and babies march out.
There are babies in our heads
not even born yet. But how we father them!
There are babies in the eyes of lovers
who reach in their thumbs and pull out babies.
And sometimes the world is not ready
and babies pile up, and the streets are full
of babies, and boxes are full of babies,
and sacks, and garbage cans,
and broken down cars are full of babies.
And they are taken home to play with Hunger,
who doesn't play fair and should be sent home
himself, but who wins all the games,
placing himself like a god in the eyes
of those who must worship him.
Or they are taken by the shorter route
and cut off at the pass. And there are babies
for bottles and autopsies, babies for war
and abandonment, and some left over.
There are plenty of babies, no shortages foreseen.

from The Apprentice Grave Digger

9.

I killed a king snake sunning
in the branches of a cedar,
cut him with a spade
until he spilled
his breakfast on the grass.

Five sparrow babies,
slick and sweet,
poured out like heavy jam,
the fruit still warm.

I nudged them in the grave.
The snake, the birds, the man,
together in the ground.

10.

When it rains
we bury ourselves
in piles of plastic grass,

in the shed,
with straps and shovels,
and visions of the dead.

11.

I don't like to dig
the children's graves.
They cramp you in,
not room enough
to swing your axe
or work a sweat.

I'd like to climb in,
brace my back,
and push them longer.
If I was stronger.

12.

"What do you do?"

I build holes in the ground.

The Beekeeper's Wife

She wakes beside his body brown as bees.
Why can't he know? She wonders as she waits
why loneliness must be a private thing.
If she could send the messages she keeps
her hands would tell him of her aching bones,
her mouth would be the only sound he knows.
Outside, the queen is dead, the shifting trees
are warm with bees and ripple with the wind
of wings. Oh she would be the keeper's girl
and run with lifted skirts to gather them,
and hang her heart upon a leaf-blown tree
to house them in, and feed them on her blood.

But could she bear the weight of their blind love?
Some nights she thinks the sound will never stop,
or dreams the bees are netted in her hair.
One day she saw them fill a calf's skull, bring
the bleached bones back to life, become the eyes,
the living tongue that cries. Why can't he see
her body is alive? Why won't he wake
to heal her given wounds? She moves along the bed
and touches him, and waits for him to know
the torture of her fingers, where they go.
There is a fluid movement to his sleep.
She feels his body swarm across the sheet.

Charles Simic

Dismantling the Silence

Take down its ears first
Carefully so they don't spill over.
With a sharp whistle slit its belly open.
If there are ashes in it, close your eyes
And blow them whichever way the wind is pointing.
If there's water, sleeping water,
Bring the root of a plant that hasn't drunk for a month.

When you reach the bones,
And you haven't got a pack of dogs with you,
And you haven't got a pine coffin
And a wagon pulled by oxen to make them rattle,
Slip them quickly under your skin,
Next time you pick up your sack,
You'll hear them setting your teeth on edge. . .

It is now completely dark.
Slowly and with patience
Feel its heart. You will need to haul
A heavy chest of drawers
Into its emptiness
To make it creak
On its wheel.

Stone Inside a Stone

1

They will not turn into seed.
On the border of nothing and nothing.

Fossils of the wind.
But what wind?

You can't step twice in the same river—
With a stone you can take your sweet time.

Going to pick a flower in its heart
Is like taking a live chicken out of a bottle.

My stones will not sing the song yours are singing.

They say: everything is so simple. Touch it.
You awake in one, fall asleep in another.

Who, while the night is still deep, awakes the roosters?
A stone among us is taking notes.

The opposite has ceased to be imaginary.
There are two of us now but o what solitude.

2

Touch again. You've touched a lightning.
The thunder is still to come.

Once in my hand
The fingers speak to it in its own language.

Stone, you come from a long line of fire-thieves.
I answered your questions
Until your hardness entered my voice.
Now they can carve whatever tool they please.

This is bread never-sown, never-reaped.

Two of them hang in death's testicles.

Strength that wishes to contract
Until it resembles itself more fully.

I hear the steps of the stone.
I lift them with my tongue
To keep myself in shape
For an unknown time.

Forest

My time is coming. Once again
My trees will swing their heavy bells.

My termites, my roots and streams
Will stitch their chill into the heart of man
Laying out my most ancient trail.

I speak of the north, of its pull
Stuck in my mouth like a bit.

Whoever looks now in the palm of his hand
Will notice the imprints of strange flowers
I have preserved in my rocks.

I will bare bones to tell fortunes by,
Snow with tracks of all the fabled highwaymen.
Ladies and gentlemen, you will hear a star
Dead a million years, in the throat of a bird.

The human body will be revealed for what it is—
A cluster of roots
Pulling in every direction.

There'll be plenty of time
When an acorn grows out of your ear
To accustom yourself to my ways,
To carve yourself a hermit's toothpick.

Bestiary for the Fingers of My Right Hand

1

Thumb, loose tooth of a horse.
Rooster to his hens.
Horn of a devil. Fat worm
They have attached to my flesh
At the time of my birth.
It takes four to hold him down,
Bend him in half, until the bone
Begins to whimper.

Cut him off. He can take care
Of himself. Take root in the earth,
Or go hunting with wolves.

2

The second points the way.
True way. The path crosses the earth,
The moon and some stars.
Watch, he points further.
He points to himself.

3

The middle one has backache.
Stiff, still unaccustomed to this life;
An old man at birth. It's about something
That he had and lost,
That he looks for within my hand,
The way a dog looks
For fleas
With a sharp tooth.

4

The fourth is mystery.
Sometimes as my hand
Rests on the table
He jumps by himself
As though someone called his name.

After each bone, finger,
I come to him, troubled.

5

Something stirs in the fifth
Something perpetually at the point
Of birth. Weak and submissive,
His touch is gentle.
It weighs a tear.
It takes the mote out of the eye.

Poem

Every morning I forget how it is.
I watch the smoke mount
In great strides above the city.
I belong to no one.

Then, I remember my shoes,
How I have to put them on,
How bending over to tie them up
I will look into the earth.

Gary Snyder

By the Tama River at the North End of the Plain in April

Round smooth stones
up here in the weeds
the air a grey wet,

Across the Tama river
a screen drum turns sorting gravel:
dumping loads in
dump trucks one by one.

Deep in the hills
the water might be clean

Grilling raw squid over smoky twigs
a round screen perched on broken bricks

Masa bending on the rocks
Staring close to the water,
Nanao and Nagasawa
with their lifted cups of shochu,

Friends and poets
Eating, drinking in the rain,
and these round river stones.

It Was When

We harked up the path in the dark
to the bamboo house
green strokes down my back
arms over your doubled hips
under cow-breath thatch
bent cool
breasts brush my chest
—and Naga walked in with a candle,
"I'm sleepy"

Or jungle ridge by a snag—
banyan canyon—a Temminck's Robin
whirled down the waterfall gorge
in zazen, a poncho spread out on the stones.
below us the overturning
silvery
brush-bamboo slopes—
rainsqualls came up on us naked
brown nipples in needles of ocean-
cloud
rain.

Or the night in the farmhouse
with Franco on one side, or Pon
Miko's head against me, I swung you
around and came into you
careless and joyous,
late
when Antares had set

Or out on the boulders
south beach at noon
rockt by surf
burnd under by stone
burnd over by sun
saltwater caked
skin swing
hips on my eyes

burn between;

That we caught: sprout
	took grip in your womb and it held.
	new power in your breath called its place.
	blood of the moon	stoppt;
	you pickt your steps well.

Waves
	and the
		prevalent easterly
			breeze.
		whispering into you,
			through us,
				the grace.

Kai, Today

A teen-age boy in training pants
        stretching by the river
A girl child weeping, climbing
        up her elder sister;
The Kawaramachi Beggar's steady look and
        searching reach of gritty hand
        in plastic sidewalk pail
                with lip of grease

                these fates.

        before Masa and I met
What's your from-the-beginning face?
        Kai.
        born again
To the Mother's hoarse bear-down
        groan and dark red mask:
        spiralling, glistening, blue-white, up

And out from her
                (dolphins leaping in threes
                through blinding silver inter-
                faces, Persian
                Gulf tanker's wave-slip
                opening, boundless
                        whap
                as they fall back,
                arcing
                into her—)

                    sea.

William Stafford

Willows

Every one
has to learn
humility.

Say they settle
on an island:
floods take them—

They have to swim,
a few stragglers,
to a bend

On the shore.
There against
the barbed wire

They have to stand
in cold light
and begin

To oppose
everything.
They become

Their own kind—
ancestors,
bent again

In slow relief,
their incredible
years-long ballet

Lithe at first,
till they bow
—absolute—

All the way.

On Earth

In Wyoming, high, often cold or
hot, you can walk the curve of the world
always varied with a slope for you,
where by crouching or even lying flat
in one of its hollows you have shade
or a huddle in the sun, out of the wind,
as coyotes or badgers do, taking their
riches full length, bathed in the immediate,
walled around by that constant whisper
the world makes passing its eons,
occasionally fluting a little streaming
note—a rock, or you, noticed by the wind.

Memorandum

You'll see some time—half
of the world will fracture
or you will come out on a cold
ridge, flashed into knowing, and find
how all over our state, better
than we deserved, stories
went on, millions of unbound
sagas the wise were too dumb
to find: the shivering wolves
aflame in their savagery, hedges
that wove God's lost garlands
around abandoned fields.

Maybe a man lived somewhere—consider—
down in his yard, vicious, in the trash
and low schemes, but all of his life
by his door, unmerited, a fir tree
grew; at the top whole generations
of beautiful birds lived and sang.

All over our state, all over
the world, spiders are weaving,
rodents pause, whole forests
lean at once. And only some of the
things that shine are mean.

At First National

Every morning when day
crosses the street a calendar
flips over in the bank.
Pennies pooch out
the vault and roll into someone
else's account, and from all
fields corn and wheat
flow to dribble the ledger
where machines peck "Amen"
over the crops.

Somewhere the dust meets
to discuss the manager—how
in December he
always tightens fences in Wyoming
and sends deep-footed snowmen
to stop all payments in Michigan.

Later it is the meeting
to forgive him again;
of course all animals except
a few dogs vote no,
but always at the spring meeting
the states melt and vote yes, yes,
yes, with all kinds of flowers.

The Prodigal

After Shakespeare the wandering tongue
lived along hedgerows, lonesome,
never forgetting, though it came to stand
gravely in halls, or to stalk across the land
staring through windows when town folk sang.
Even today it leaps in the spring
on casual speakers caught in some rhyme
mated to a meaning, partner to time.

Mark Strand

The New Poetry Handbook

1. If a man understands a poem,
   he shall have troubles.

2. If a man lives with a poem,
   he shall die lonely.

3. If a man lives with two poems,
   he shall be unfaithful to one.

4. If a man conceives of a poem,
   he shall have one less child.

5. If a man conceives of two poems,
   he shall have two children less.

6. If a man wears a crown on his head as he writes,
   he shall be found out.

7. If a man wears no crown on his head as he writes,
   he shall deceive no one but himself.

8. If a man gets angry at a poem,
   he shall be scorned by men.

9. If a man continues to be angry at a poem,
   he shall be scorned by women.

10. If a man publicly denounces poetry,
    his shoes will fill with urine.

11. If a man gives up poetry for power,
    he shall have lots of power.

12. If a man brags about his poems,
    he shall be loved by fools.

13. If a man brags about his poems and loves fools,
he shall write no more.

14. If a man denies his poems pleasure,
his wit shall wear boots.

15. If a man craves attention because of his poems,
he shall be like a jackass in moonlight.

16. If a man writes a poem and praises the poem of a
fellow,
he shall have a beautiful mistress.

17. If a man writes a poem and praises the poem of a
fellow overly,
he shall drive his mistress away.

18. If a man claims the poem of another,
his heart shall double in size.

19. If a man lets his poems go naked,
he shall fear death.

20. If a man fears death,
he shall be saved by his poems.

21. If a man does not fear death,
he may or may not be saved by his
poems.

22. If a man finishes a poem,
he shall bathe in the blank wake of his
passion
and be kissed by white paper.

Courtship

There is a girl you like so you tell her
your penis is big, but that you cannot get yourself
to use it. Its demands are ridiculous, you say,
even self-defeating, but to be honored somehow,
briefly, inconspicuously in the dark.

When she closes her eyes in horror,
you take it all back. You tell her you're almost
a girl yourself and can understand why she is shocked.
When she is about to walk away, you tell her
you have no penis, that you don't

know what got into you. You get on your knees.
She suddenly bends down to kiss your shoulder and you know
you're on the right track. You tell her you want
to bear children and that is why you seem confused.
You wrinkle your brow and curse the day you were born.

She tries to calm you, but you lose control.
You reach for her panties and beg forgiveness as you do.
She squirms and you howl like a wolf. Your craving
seems monumental. You know you will have her.
Taken by storm, she is the girl you will marry.

James Tate

Barrels of Wedding Rings

Barrels of wedding rings
on the streetcorner: enlist
everyone you can to help
collect; just pull them
off and carry as many
as you can to the nearest
barrel. There will be
someone around to answer
questions at first if
you should not fully
understand the procedure.

The main thing is time—
do not waste a lot of time
guessing the value and
size, etc. because there
will be thousands; later
will be even more difficult
when we record the names
and initials and verses
engraved inside. Barrels
spilling over with wedding
rings: we will need more

and more barrels: enlist
everyone you can. And
do not feel responsible
for my rage, though strangely
enough it was directed
at you for a brief time.

Up Here

The motel was made for love
as you were. I undressed you
with grace and tenderness,
kissing each newly bared part.

There you lay, your small, white
body throbbing in my hand
like a bird. We were silent.
The right word was not needed.

Supple. What was I doing
suddenly pacing around
the bed, scratching my head,
staring down at your gaze up
at me? *Recognition.*

I would not call you *svelte.*
Your breasts were barely a hand-
ful; I like small breasts, which fit
a hand. Your thighs were a feast,
though, and, walking, now and then
I would dip down to nibble
them. They were good: *wholesome.*
They were the bread of life.

Now your lips are moving, now
your hands reach up at me.
I feel as if I might be one
or two thousand feet above you.
Your lips form something, a bubble,

which rises and rises into
my hand: inside it is a word:
Help. I would like to help,
believe me, but up here nothing
is possible, nothing is clear:
Help. Help me.

Fire Dance

In your eyes, I am a wealth of sin:
you see me with kegs of cognac,
harems of nubile lovers
bathing me in sweet smelling oil.
You see me smoking opium
in the early hours, drowsy,

nibbling at a quail's wing
and a naked girl. O once in a while
I roll over and dictate a poem:
I smile graciously at this
charming act of condescension
and my thirty-three wives applaud

quietly. The next day it appears
in the New Yorker and I donate
the paltry reward to the veterans
of the Turko-Cuban Civil War
or the survivors of the Flemish
fire sale. Yes, Sister Michele,

it is all true: the fire-dance
you are waiting for in the next
life happens every night
on my livingroom floor:
I writhe and read and write
until almost dawn until

there is not a light on
in the world and the ghosts
of beauty have disappeared
and my pride has crossed over
into complete shame and
emptiness and the thrush says
sleep you goddamned fool.

The Blue Booby

The blue booby lives
on the bare rocks
of Galapagos
and fears nothing.
It is a simple life:
they live on fish,
and there are few predators.
Also, the males do not
make fools of themselves
chasing after the young
ladies. Rather,
they gather the blue
objects of the world
and construct from them

a nest—an occasional
Gaulois package,
a string of beads,
a piece of cloth from
a sailor's suit. This
replaces the need for
dazzling plumage;
in fact, in the past
fifty million years
the male has grown
considerably duller,
nor can he sing well.
The female, though,
asks little of him—

the blue satisfies her
completely, has
a magical effect
on her. When she returns
from her day of
gossip and shopping,
she sees he has found her
a new shred of blue foil:
for this she rewards him
with her dark body,
the stars turn slowly
in the blue foil beside them
like the eyes of a mild savior.

Peter Wild

Kite Man

We first met our next-door neighbor
rounding the corner of his house
with a kite;
he smiled and nodded,
blurted his name,
but it trailed off in the
wind as he ran . . .

beyond that we've never met him,
but have become used
to his flashing by the windows
with his kite,
his feet thumping across the wet lawns
at night;

he appears an amiable man, sweatered,
and standing far off in the fields
watching his kite
soar and sip in the spring winds;
and once by chance
I saw it hanging
magnified against the eye of the moon . . .

occasionally we see his family
staring from the window,
his children sunken-eyed,
and his wife's fingers white
upon the sill;
I've called to him,
but he only nods and smiles,
floundering through drifts, tugging
the icy kite,
looking back over his shoulder as he runs,
lips and fingers turning blue . . .

Quitobaquito

they sleep beneath the trees
knives in their mouths
to protect them from naked women
and evil dreams;
but lying on their backs
they can still hear the gritty wind
rasping through their heads
like screams
through the grates of empty cells. . .
even here beneath the cottonwoods
afraid to open their eyes
and see smiling ladies
holding their huge breasts open
and devils making obscene
gestures above them
in the round dark arches of the trees. . .

devils,
who have followed them
dancing across the fiery plains
and flashed wet-backed
in the blackness
around their camps—
they had seen the splayed
footprints in the sand—
perhaps, consumed by flames,
had followed them here, too,
to lie in the darkness on their bellies
in the slime
and suck water from the pools
through their long snouts. . .
the horses smell them
and tear their lips on the bit
and refuse to eat the grass;

and when the ducks stir
in the middle of the night
leap wild to their feet
seizing their crosses
and their swords,
and awake
blinded by the sun,
bodies sore from tossing
on the stony ground;
kneel on the wet banks
rubbing their faces raw
in the pools. . .
and filling up the long water bags
clench their teeth
as they enter the waste
of splintered rock,
the sun already beating on their backs.

Haystacks

Across the plains they slump
one behind the other,
backs to the moon;
chins sunk to breastplates
lances pointed to the ground

astride horses which have forgotten
the command to move on.

sleeping in their armor,
                they themselves
cannot recall what the word was

once it passed through their minds
                like a wandering moth,
but disappeared
          before they could grasp it,

and now on their backs they can feel
                                only vaguely
slender fingers caressing metal,
the damp air
          eating into their joints

An Apology for Wolves

I.

They have always
vilified us,
sensing our stealth
and their lack of it,

and moved by the first impulse
of their dim minds,
throw stones, beat shields,
catch us in their iron sights. . .

as if we wanted their women
or would steal their Gods. . .

II.

it is true, we've been caught
on occasion with the remnants
of petticoats still in our mouths,
or sporting a red cap, just for a lark.

but we've got a bad press
which capitalizes on such exceptions:
a grandmother or two
coughed up now and then,

and doesn't consider
our loss of face
when driven into the suburbs
by a long winter and heavy snows.

III.

actually, it's just a simple lack
of understanding—on their part,
a myopia common
to all muscular animals. . .

we mean no harm
but must pursue
that fine exhilaration
instinctively ours:

flaming tails in bushes
and leaves slipping along our backs.

John Woods

Gloss

from Gen. Leslie R. Groves'
Now It Can Be Told: The Story of the Manhattan Project

1.

"Whatever you may
accomplish,
you will incur the everlasting
enmity
of the entire Northwest
if you harm a single
scale
on a single salmon."

At Hanford,
the Columbia River
cooled the reactors.
Asphalt was poured to protect
the typists' heels.
Morale was high
in the motor pool.

At Los Alamos, General Groves
bought a boys' boarding school
whose teachers were serving elsewhere.
Its owners were happy to sell out
"and close down for the duration—
and, as it turned out, forever."

Hiroshima
Nagasaki
no scales injured
except a few goldfish
101,000 dead
128,000 injured
more or less for the duration,
and, as it turned out,
forever.

Forever it turns out
the target must be large enough
to contain the anger.
Nothing to be learned
from a hole.
Some cities were too small,
others already burning,
Kyoto had culture.

Hiroshima had everything
including American POW's.

2.

"Not one was hired
or kept on who had been convicted of rape,

arson,

or narcotics charges.
Such people were felt to be
unreliable
because of their demonstrated weakness
in moral fiber
and their liability to blackmail."

What's a little rape, General?
It shows a crude affection,
something to be learned from a hole,
no scales injured,
cools down those reactors
in the typist's heels.

And arson is really too much.

No weak fiber
in the blackmail
of the Bomb.

All our teachers were serving elsewhere.

3.

Truman thought long into the night.
General Groves thought long into the night.
The Pentagon thought five ways from the middle.

There was uncertainty about the location
of Heisenberg.

Otto Hahn had "contemplated suicide
when he first saw
the full potentialities of his discovery . . .
After bracing himself
with alcoholic stimulants
he became calmer . . ."

Einstein
Groves
Fermi
Truman
DuPont
ushered in the atomic age.

General Groves: "I personally thought of Blondin
crossing Niagara Falls on his tightrope . . ."

Teller was pregnant.

"As General Eisenhower put it, 'I have so many things
to deal with that it puts an undue burden on me to be
given any secret information, as I am then forced to

think
constantly about
what
is secret
and what
is not.' "

The Night of Even Breathing

In this night of even breathing,
I am awake, but through my wife,
my sons, the halls and piano
moves the sound of even breathing.
From the heater, the open eyes
of three guitars, in books
and saved string, the night
of even breathing spins steadily.

The house breathes through its pores,
the attic vents, a slow breath,
deep pulse. Some waters move
a little in the walls, and lightning
turns over dreamily in the meter.

So the town breathes, the trees
lean down a little, the grass heavy.
Only the lovers, the dying,
and the bloodhunting owl
make red flowers on a black vine,
the long vine of even breathing.

Just Before Morning

The cutting bar rusts
in a dark corner.
The scythe no longer gathers the moon.
A banty hen trails her seven chicks
down the dry stream,
up under the new peach trees.
The geese and the old collie
have reached an understanding
about the long grass under the arbor.
The potatoes think deeply about starch
there, in the garden,
but they'll grow up to be village idiots.

Just before the sun rolls up
my father steps out in the wet grass,
listening four ways.
He'd be hard to surprise.

Soon the cows will complain about milk.
They'll come down, the pup
skating school figures under their hooves.
The bull on the next farm
will lean on the wire, singing.
And the air will gather in the willow,
leveling out, pushing these thoughts,
like torn pieces of New Deal posters
through weeds and dark stones.

Charles Wright

The Poet Grows Older

It seemed, at the time, so indifferent an age that I recall nothing of it except an infinite tedium to be endured. I envied no one, nor dreamed of anything in particular as, unwillingly, I enveloped myself in all of the various disguises of a decent childhood. Nothing now comes to mind of ever embarking upon famous voyages to the usual continents; of making, from the dark rooms and empty houses of my imagination, brilliant escapes from unnatural enemies; or, on rainy winter afternoons in an attic, of inventing one plot or counterplot against a prince or a beast . . . Instead, it must have been otherwise.

I try to remember, nevertheless, something of all that time and place, sitting alone here in a room in the middle of spring, hearing the sound of a rain which has fallen for most of April, concerned with such different things, things done by others . . . I read of the aimless coups in the old dynasties from Africa to Afghanistan, their new republics whose lists of war lords alone are enough to distress the Aryan tongue; of intricate rockets in search of a planet, soon, perhaps, to land in a country somewhere outside the pedestrian reach of reason; of the latest, old sailor's account of a water dragon seen bathing off the grizzled coast of Scotland . . . It is at times such as this, and without thinking, really, clothed in my goat's-wool robes, that I steal a camel from an outlying Arabian stable, gather together my clansmen, and gallop for days along the miraculous caravan trails to Asia.

from The Bolivar Letters

5.

It is not, you understand, the bat,
That blind squeaker, I hear in the dark;
It is not, like a murmur of voices, the frog
Hidden within the oak—rather,
It is the owl, in his silent washings,
Floating across the moon,
Trailing his shadow like a change in the weather:
Over the fields, over the wall,
Over the low parts of the garden until
It enters, at last, the trees
Where it breaks into edges, edges that
Scatter along the leaves, resemble
The loose connections starting to drift, now,
Like cold seeds
                                just under my skin.

from The Bolivar Letters

10.

The leaves sink in the pool.
The leaves sink in the pool
Unpatterned, and cover the bottom.
They lie there, unmoving,
Without so much as a sigh.

On the pool's surface, insects
Are trundled about by the wind.

But wait! Like a clot of blood,
Working its way downward, a pome
From the pyracanthus drops toward the leaves.

Between the leaves and the insects,
Where the pome falls, the water
Is turning in on itself, over and over,
As though with a pure delight.

Piccola Elegia

L. G.: Requiescat . . .

Nicky, the word has come to the west coast
Of how you
Shuffled your feet, stammered,
And slipped out the back door

When no one was looking.
What did you have in mind?

* * *

I picture myself back there,
In the kitchen, peering out
Through the glass, then through the orchard, your shirt

A small red dot among
The apple trees that run down
The long slope: the water
Glitters and flashes in

The cold sunlight; I try
To open the window, to tell you
To wait, to come back, but
It is too late, too
Late in the day; already

The boat is adrift; it is
On fire; the flames
Splash at the gunwales; and you
Are smoke, Nicky, you are smoke.

Entries

– The seepage from what you have killed in one part of
your life will rise, eventually, through your rooms
no matter what doors you might try to close.

– Always it is the same dark you touch, wherever you
touch, its odors, its watery flesh closing about you,
spreading across your hands like new skin.

– What *does* one say to the mad? They hang from their
trees like swollen fruit, unwilling to fall, untouched
by the weather. What meetings can hold them there?
What candor?

– The shed skin, the broken rind, your life but a catch
now in your own throat . . .

– So one has to dive, sinking more rapidly than what
sinks in advance of you: once down, once under it
all, the quieter it becomes, the less fearful it
becomes, the quieter it becomes.

Crescent Bay Beach

David Young

Two for the Hampton Institute

Based on photographs from the Hampton Album, taken by Frances B. Johnston, 1900.

1

The class is judging swine.

We are afraid that the mud
Will soil their grandmother dresses
And union soldier uniforms.

The teacher, who looks like a chauffeur,
Points to the loafing pigs
And the class follows his gaze,

But a turn-of-the-century swine
Looks out from under his ears
In our direction.

"This beautiful dream," he says . . .
Old leaves blow past.
A windmill spins in the distance.

2

The history class on the cliff
Inspects the great black cannon.
An iron whale in the sunlight,
It can fire into the sea.

The tough grass holds our shadow
As we step back to view
The cluster of dark learners
Posed in the line of fire.

In the background the sea remains
The sea, immense and restless.
There are no thoughts in the air;
Impossibly pale: the sky

The Boxcar Poem

The boxcars drift by
clanking
they have their own
speech on scored
wood their own
calligraphy
Soo Line
they say in meadows
Lackawanna quick at crossings
Northern Pacific, a
nightmurmur, Northern
Pacific

even empty
they carry
in dark corners
among smells of wood and sacking
the brown wrappings of sorrow
the rank straw of revolution
the persistence of war

and often
as they roll past
like weathered obedient
angels you can see
right through them
to yourself
in a bright
field, a crow
on either shoulder.

The Owl

You know this dream. You move
down a moon road in a clouded
flower-heavy night; the grim
daylight terrors slumber:
missiles doze in their silos,
government fists uncurl, assassins
shelve their guns, the cops
sleep in their stink like bears,
Asians, Indians, Negroes,
cease their tunneling, the trucks
lie in the fields on their backs,
even the softball towns are stunned
and the farms gone back to grass.

Beautiful! All fireflies, buffalo
hills, a snow of love on the senses,
the tight labyrinths of time
turning to lowland mist, but
what is this owl come out of your head
to climb and hang, all talons and beak
two hundred yards overhead in the dark?
One thing is sure; he won't
slide in as easy as he got out,
he'll have to drop, hooks first,
into your stirring hair,
shatter and gouge his way
back to his perch . . .

The night quivers. After all
you are no more than a meal.
You stumble, arms out. The owl
begins his plunge. Now,
for the first time you hear
the celebrations in the distance:
bonfires you lit as a child
rabbits and savages, laughing, dancing.

In Heaven

There
where the self is a fine powder
drifting free

There you can be
by simple wish
whatever you like:
a fish swiped by a bear's paw
a woman whose son is insane
a spear in the side of a tiger

They do not feast there
or seek the ecstasies of love
they do not hymn perfection

For their own reasons
they care most
to assume the shapes of suffering:

helicopters swooning into clearings
through crossfire, burning

or an old hare
limping across
a stripped field
in late November.

Biographical Notes

Ai's poems have appeared in *Lillabulero* and *Intro* under the name Florence Anthony. She is from Tucson, Arizona, and writes of herself: "My mother cast me out of her belly in the seventh month of pregnancy on October 21, 1947. I had a hard life, I'm still alive."

Michael Benedikt has two books of poetry, *The Body* and *Sky*, both published by Wesleyan University Press, and is working on a book of prose poems, *Universe*. He is a widely published editor and translator of poetry and drama, as well as a critic of the visual arts. Benedikt was born in 1937 and lives with his wife in New York City. He has received a Guggenheim Fellowship for his poetry.

Robert Bly, 45, edits and publishes *The Seventies* magazine and The Seventies Press books. His books of poetry are *Silence in the Snowy Fields*, *The Light Around the Body* (National Book Award, 1967), and *The Morning Glory*. He recently completed his first play, *The Worm Is My Shepherd, I Shall Not Want*, and is close to finishing a new book of poetry, including poems in this volume. Beacon Press published his long-planned anthology, *Forty Poems Touching on Recent American History*, in August 1970.

Richard Brautigan published several small books of poetry in limited editions and then collected them in one volume, *The Pill Versus the Springhill Mine Disaster*, published first by Four Seasons Foundation and then by Delacorte. He has also published three novels and a book of new poems, *Rommel Drives On Deep into Egypt*. Brautigan is 36 and has lived in San Francisco for many years.

Philip Dacey has published widely in the "littles," as he calls them, and has two chapbooks out from small presses in Wisconsin. He was born in 1939 and has taught at Stanford University, the

University of Iowa, the University of Missouri at St. Louis, and Miles College, and is currently teaching in the Writers' Workshop at Southwest Minnesota State College.

Glover Davis was born in 1939. He grew up in California, served in the Navy, and studied in the Writers' Workshop at the University of Iowa. He now teaches poetry at San Diego State College in California, and lives in a trailer in the East San Diego Mountains. The Cummington Press published his first book of poems, *Bandaging Bread*, in late 1970.

Russell Edson writes short plays, prose pieces, prose poems, and poems, from his home in Stamford, Connecticut. He is the author of *The Very Thing That Happens* (New Directions), and a recent book of poems from The Jargon Society, *What A Man Can See.*

John Haines lived for many years as a homesteader in Alaska before moving recently to the California central coast. His first book of poems, *Winter News*, was published by Wesleyan University Press; a new book of poems, *The Stone Harp*, including poems in this volume, will be published by Wesleyan in 1971. Haines is 47 and has received a Guggenheim Fellowship for his poetry.

Michael Harper was born in Brooklyn in 1938, and was raised there and in Los Angeles. He attended California State College at Los Angeles and the Writers' Workshop at the University of Iowa. His first book of poems, *Dear John, Dear Coltrane*, was published by the University of Pittsburgh Press, and a second book of poems, *History Is Your Own Heartbeat*, will be published Spring 1971 by the University of Illinois Press. He is married and has two sons.

Robert L. Jones, 28, was born in California, and has lived in California, Texas, and Michigan. He is presently teaching in the English Department at Western Michigan University in Kalamazoo, and he is married. Poems of his have appeared in *Southern Review, North American Review, TransPacific*, and in the anthology, *Down at the Santa Fe Depot.*

Galway Kinnell was born in 1927 in Providence, Rhode Island, and makes his home in Sheffield, Vermont. He has translated Villon, Yves Bonnefoy, and Yvan Goll, and has written one novel, *Black Light*, and three books of poetry, *What A Kingdom It Was, Flower Herding on Mount Monadnock*, and *Body Rags*. His *First Poems* appeared in 1970. His two poems in this anthology are sections from a book-length poem not yet finished.

Philip Levine is the author of four books of poetry, *On the Edge, Not This Pig,* and two recent collections, *5 Detroits* (Unicorn Press) and *Thistles* (Turret Books, London); his poems in this volume are from a new book he is working on. Levine was born in Detroit in 1928, and lives with his wife and three sons in California. He has received the Joseph Henry Jackson Award and grants from the Chapelbrook Foundation for his poetry.

Larry Levis was born in Selma, California, in 1946, and grew up in the San Joaquin Valley in central California. He has an MA Degree in creative writing from Syracuse University, currently teaches at California State College at Los Angeles, and is married. His poems have appeared in *Intro, Unicorn Journal, Nickel Review,* and *Syracuse Poems 1963-1969*.

Lou Lipsitz writes: "Born early on Saturday morning, late in October, 1938 in Brooklyn. First discovered poetry in junior high school library reading Robert Frost's 'The Road Not Taken' which reminded me of something I'd already lost. Guess what? *Cold Water*, Wesleyan, 1967. Now teach at U. of North Carolina, work on studying politics. Involved in the Caucus for a New Political Science. Slowly concluding poetry is far less important than I used to believe. Note to Robert Bly: Joy is not all there is in the unconscious."

Paul Malanga, 27, was born and raised in Tucson, Arizona. He attended the University of Arizona, the University of Washington, and now teaches at Oregon College of Education. With Bobby Byrd, he edited the poetry magazine, *From A Window*. He appears in the recent anthology, *Inside Outer Space*, is married, and is an itinerant rock and roll guitarist.

James McMichael was born in Pasadena, California, in 1939. He went to school at the University of California, Santa Barbara, and at Stanford University and is currently teaching in The Writing Center at the University of California, Irvine. His first book of poems, *Against the Falling Evil*, will appear in 1971 from Swallow Press.

W. S. Merwin is the prolific author of many books of poetry and translation. Recent volumes of translation include *Voices* (from Antonio Porchia), *Transparence of the World* (selected poems of Jean Follain), and *Selected Translations 1948-1968*. His poems appearing here are from a new book, *The Carrier of Ladders*, published Fall 1970. Merwin is 44, lives in France, and taught recently at Columbia University.

Bert Meyers, 42, has worked as a warehouseman, janitor, and housepainter, and for ten years as a picture-framer and gilder. He teaches at Pitzer College in Claremont, California, is married, and has two children. His first book of poems, *Early Rain*, was published by Alan Swallow, and a second book of poems, *The Dark Birds*, by Doubleday. Meyers has been the recipient of grants and awards from the Ingram Merrill Foundation and the National Endowment in the Arts for his poetry.

Robert Mezey, 36, lives in the Sierra Nevada Mountains in California, with his wife and two children. He is the co-editor of *Naked Poetry*, the recently published anthology of American free verse, and the author of five books of poetry, the most recent, *The Door Standing Open: New and Selected Poems 1954-1969*, published by Oxford University Press, and in this country by Houghton Mifflin.

Dennis Saleh was born in Chicago in 1942, and raised in Fresno, California. He attended Fresno State College, the University of Arizona, and the University of California, Irvine, and has taught poetry at the University of California, Santa Cruz. Saleh is married and has one son. A small collection of his poems, *A Guide to Familiar American Incest*, will be published Fall 1971 by Triskelion Press.

Herbert Scott, 40, is married and the father of five children he had when he received his MFA Degree from the University of Iowa Writers' Workshop. He has taught in schools in Iowa and Missouri, and most recently in Michigan. He has completed a book of poems, *The Apprentice Grave Digger*, and has been a contributor to *Harper's, Poetry, North American Review,* and *Beloit Poetry Journal.*

Charles Simic was born in 1938, and is a graduate of New York University. He has published two books of poetry, *What the Grass Says* and *Somewhere Among Us A Stone Is Taking Notes*, with Kayak Books, and will have a new collection out in 1971, from George Braziller. Simic is currently teaching at Hayward State College in California.

Gary Snyder was born in San Francisco in 1930. His books of poetry are *Riprap, Myths and Texts, A Range of Poems, Rivers and Mountains Without End, The Back Country*, and *Regarding Wave*. He recently published *Earth House Hold*, a book of essays and journal entries. Snyder is married and has two sons.

William Stafford has written four books of poetry, and received the National Book Award for his second collection, *Traveling Through the Dark*. His most recent collection, *Allegiances*, was published in April 1970. Stafford was born in Kansas in 1914 and has taught for many years at Lewis and Clark College in Oregon. He is married and the father of four children.

Mark Strand was born in Summerside, Prince Edward Island, Canada, in 1934. He attended Antioch College and Yale University, where he now teaches. He has published three collections of poetry, *Sleeping With One Eye Open, Reasons for Moving*, and *Darker*, and is editor of *The Contemporary American Poets*. He is currently writing a book on the painter, Edward Hopper.

James Tate was born in Kansas City in 1943. He has taught at the University of Iowa, the University of California, Berkeley, Columbia University, and Emerson College. His books of poems include *The Lost Pilot, Notes of Woe, The Torches, Row With Your Hair, Shepherds of the Mist*, and *The Oblivion Ha-Ha*. He is editor, with Charles Simic, of *Gotteman's Curse*, A Magazine With No Past and No Future.

Peter Wild has published widely in magazines of all sizes, shapes, and kinds. He has several small books and pamphlets of poetry, including *Sonnets, Mica Mtn Poems*, and *Terms and Renewals*, and a full-length collection, *The Afternoon in Dismay*, published by the Art Association of Cincinnati. Wild, 31, is married and has spent the last several years in the Southwest, lately living and teaching in Texas.

John Woods has written four books of poetry, the most recent, *Keeping Out of Trouble*. He is 45, married, and teaches in Michigan. He writes: "I have not been given a Guggenheim, Rockefeller or Ford Fellowship. I have not read at the YMHA in New York. I appear in neither of the Two Anthologies which explain the Fifties, etc., but I have the poems."

Charles Wright was born in Pickwick Dam, Tennessee, in 1935 and now lives in Laguna Beach, California. He teaches in The Writing Center at the University of California, Irvine, and has published one book of poems, *The Grave of the Right Hand*, Wesleyan University Press, 1970. He is married to an ex-movie star.

David Young was born in Davenport, Iowa, in 1936. He attended Carleton College, Yale, and has taught at Oberlin College since 1961. His first collection of poems, *Sweating Out the Winter*, won the 1968 United States Award of the International Poetry Forum, and was published in the University of Pittsburgh Press Poetry Series. Young is married, has two children, and is the editor of *Field*, a poetry magazine.